Francis Willey Kelsey

List of Books Recommended For a High School Classical Library

Francis Willey Kelsey

List of Books Recommended For a High School Classical Library

ISBN/EAN: 9783744771535

Printed in Europe, USA, Canada, Australia, Japan

Cover: Foto ©Andreas Hilbeck / pixelio.de

More available books at **www.hansebooks.com**

[*Price Ten Cents*

LIST OF BOOKS

RECOMMENDED FOR A

HIGH SCHOOL CLASSICAL LIBRARY

BY A COMMITTEE OF THE

MICHIGAN SCHOOLMASTERS' CLUB

EDITED BY

CLARENCE LINTON MEADER

Instructor in Latin in the University of Michigan

WITH AN INTRODUCTORY NOTE BY

FRANCIS W. KELSEY

SECOND EDITION, REVISED

PUBLISHED FOR THE COMMITTEE BY
THE MACMILLAN COMPANY
NEW YORK
1897

NOTE TO THE FIRST EDITION

The Committee by whom the following list was selected, was appointed at the Spring Meeting of the Michigan Schoolmasters' Club, in March, 1894. (Cf. the Educational Review *for June, 1894, p. 39). It consists of the following members:* Clarence L. Meader, *Instructor in Latin in the University of Michigan,* Chairman; Professor B. L. D'Ooge, *of the Michigan State Normal School, Ypsilanti;* Principal E. C. Warriner, *of the Battle Creek High School;* Principal E. B. Sherman, *of the Bay City High School.*

Grateful acknowledgment of the Committee for much kind help in their work is due to Professors Kelsey, D'Ooge, Rolfe, *and* Drake, *of the University of Michigan;* Mr. Lawrence C. Hull, *of Lawrenceville, N. J.;* Mr. H. D. Sanders, Mr. H. F. De Cou, and Mr. George Rebec, *of the University of Michigan;* Professor Walter Miller, *of Leland Stanford University;* Professor Isaac B. Burgess, *of Morgan Park, Ill.;* Professor Alfred Gudeman, *University of Pennsylvania;* Professor Sidney G. Ashmore, *Union College;* Professor C. M. Moss, *University of Illinois;* Professor Walter Bridgman, *Lake Forest University;* Professor Charles Forster Smith, *University of Wisconsin;* Mr. W. W. Bishop, *Northwestern University Academy, Evanston, Ill.;* Professors S. J. Axtell and Samuel Brooks, *of Kalamazoo College;* Principal S. O. Hartwell, *of the Kalamazoo High School;* Mr. Charles B. Gleason, *of Redlands, California;* Mr. W. D. Baker, *Battle Creek High School;* Mr. F. M. Townsend, *Superintendent of Schools, Marshall, and* Principal Ralph Garwood, *Marshall, Michigan.*

ANN ARBOR, MICHIGAN, May, 1895.

NOTE TO THE SECOND EDITION

The first edition of this List (3,000 copies), published by J. V. Sheehan and Company, of Ann Arbor, was exhausted in December, 1895. In response to an immediate demand a short revised list was published in the School Review *for March, 1896 (pp. 149–157).*

In the present edition the bibliographical details have been carefully revised, and the titles of several important books published in 1896–97 have been added. Thanks are due to Mr. F. H. Jordan, *Assistant Librarian of the University of Michigan, for kind assistance in the work of revision and in the proof-reading; to* Professor Kelsey *for acceding to the request to write an introduction; and to* The Macmillan Company *for publishing the List in a form so convenient and attractive.*

Gratifying evidence has come to hand that the previous Lists have been of real service to teachers in many schools. May this new edition be even more helpful in promoting the thorough and scholarly, at the same time broad and sympathetic study of the Classics!
C. L. M.

ANN ARBOR, July, 1897.

INTRODUCTORY NOTE

The principles of selection which guided the Committee in making this "List of Books recommended for a High School Classical Library" were presented by the Chairman at the Classical Conference held in Ann Arbor in March, 1895, and were set forth at some length in the *School Review* for the following June (pp. 393–396).

The past ten years have witnessed an amount of agitation in regard to educational matters that no one could have anticipated. In the various discussions concerning high school work one point has been specially prominent, that is the importance of maintaining a high standard of scholarship. The reports of committees, the pages of educational journals, and addresses at teachers' meetings in all parts of the country manifest an awakening to larger possibilities in the accomplishment of educational results in our high schools, and an increasing recognition of the necessity, not only of adequate preparation on the part of those who undertake to give instruction, but also of deliverance from the thraldom of routine teaching.

The classical teacher who goes out into school work with high ideals of scholarship and culture too often finds himself cut off from the use of an adequate library, and misses also the inspiring contact with those who are interested in the same field. He realizes that if he is to keep abreast of his work, and to make progress professionally, he must add to his attainments, and bring to his class-room the interest and didactic power that come from continual advancement in one's studies. He feels that Xenophon and the Greek poets, that Cæsar and Cicero and Virgil did not write chiefly in order to furnish to the youth of far-off ages complex and torturing exercises in parsing and composition; he believes that, while training in Latin and Greek involves the handling of forms with absolute accuracy and the acquiring of ability to read and translate with fidelity to the original and with correct expression, there is demanded also an interpretation of the Classics as literature, as history, in fine, as a manifestation of a civilization which must be grasped and interpreted in many phases if classical study is to contribute to our modern life the elevating influence of that which was best and greatest in the life of Greece and Rome. To do the kind of work that this implies, an adequate supply of books and illustrative material is needed for the use both of the instructor and of the student. To require our classical teachers, who are second to none in professional enthusiasm and devotion to their calling, to reach the standard now set before them without at the same time offering them the facilities which their work demands, is to ask them to make bricks without straw.

In many schools the topical studies conducted along with the reading of texts in the third and fourth years are a feature of prime importance in the classical work. But whether we have in mind the needs of the classes or the needs of the teacher in making preparation for the classroom, the following list of books will be found none too extensive for the use of a secondary school which desires to have the best work done in Latin and Greek. The various branches of classical philology are represented by the latest and best works; no book is mentioned the value of which has not been made clear by actual use or by careful examination. Expenditure of money for such a collection, whether it is kept in the school building or in the public library of the town, may be justified on the same grounds as the purchase of equipment for a laboratory; books are the laboratory material of the teacher of languages.

The cost of the entire collection, Mr. Meader informs me, is not far from $1,200. Probably few schools could expend that amount in the purchase of classical books at one time; but in most cases a sum ranging from fifty to two hundred dollars a year can be obtained for this purpose either by direct appropriation, or from the proceeds of entertainments, or by subscription; thus in a few years the whole can be secured. Most schools already have the nucleus of a classical library; if one were to start from the beginning, the first fifty dollars (allowing for the usual discount from list prices), might profitably be expended for the following books: Kiepert, *Atlas Antiquus;* Liddell and Scott, *Greek-English Lexicon;* Harpers' *Latin Dictionary;* Gow, *Companion to School Classics;* Schreiber, *Atlas of Classical Antiquities; Harper's Dictionary of Classical Literature and Antiquities;* Jevons, *Greek Literature;* Cruttwell, *Roman Literature;* Curtius, *History of Greece;* Mommsen, *History of Rome;* Fowler, *Julius Cæsar;* Strachan-Davidson, *Cicero;* Sellar, *Roman Poets of the Augustan Age —Virgil;* Jebb, *Homer.* After works of a general or encyclopædic character have been secured the order of purchase is subject to so great variation, on account of differences in individual taste and methods of instruction, that it is not worth while to make specific recommendations. The titles in the List are given with so much detail that the scope and character of each book can readily be seen.

FRANCIS W. KELSEY.

LIST OF BOOKS

RECOMMENDED FOR A

HIGH SCHOOL CLASSICAL LIBRARY

I. BOOKS OF REFERENCE, HANDBOOKS, ETC.

Kiepert, H., Atlas antiquus. Twelve Maps of the Ancient World for Schools and Colleges. 11th edition, revised and enlarged. Boston, Leach, Shewell & Sanborn. F.* $2.00.†

Kiepert, H., et Huelsen, Ch., Formæ urbis Romæ antiquæ. Accedit nomenclator topographicus a Ch. Huelsen compositus. Berlin, Reimer, 1896. Q. 12 M. b.

Huelsen, Ch., The Roman Forum. 2 plates. Rome, Spithoever, 1892. Q. 2.50 M.

Engelmann, R., and Anderson, W. C. F., Pictorial Atlas to Homer's Iliad and Odyssey. New York, B. Westermann & Co., 1892. F. $3.00.

von Kampen, A., XV ad Cæsaris de bello Gallico commentarios tabulæ. Series I. *of* Descriptiones nobilissimorum apud classicos locorum. Gotha, J. Perthes, 1879. O. 1.80 M.

Oehler, R., Bilder-Atlas zu Cæsars Büchern de bello Gallico. [*Over 100 illustrations and 7 maps.*] Leipzig, Schmidt & Günther, 1890. Q. 4 M. b.

Schreiber, Th., Atlas of Classical Antiquities; edited for English use by W. C. F. Anderson, with a preface by Percy Gardner. [*101 plates, with over 1100 illustrations.*] New York, Macmillan & Co., 1895. Q. $6.50.

Baumeister, A. (*editor*), Bilder aus dem griechischen und römischen Altertum für Schüler zusammengestellt. Munich, Oldenbourg, 1889. Q. 12 M. b.

Putzger, F. W., Historischer Schul-Atlas, zur alten, mittleren und neuen Geschichte [*66 large maps, 63 accessory maps*]; revised by A. Baldamus. 21st edition. Leipzig, Velhagen & Klasing, 1896. Q. 2.70 M. b.

Liddell, H. G., and Scott, R., A Greek-English Lexicon. 7th edition, revised and enlarged. New York, Harper & Bros., 1883. Q. $10.00.

Yonge, C. D., An English-Greek Lexicon [with new articles, appendix of proper names, Pillon's Greek Synonyms, and an essay on the order of words in Attic prose by Ch. Short]; edited by H. Drisler. New York, Harper & Bros., 1886. O. $4.50.

Autenrieth, G., Homeric Dictionary for use in Schools and Colleges; translated from the German with additions and corrections by R. P. Keep. Revised edition. New York, Harper & Bros., 1891. D. $1.10.

Thayer, J. H., A Greek-English Lexicon of the New Testament. Being Grimm's Wilke's Clavis Novi Testamenti translated, revised and enlarged. New York, Harper & Bros., 1888. O. $5.00.

---

* *The following abbreviations have been employed :* F. —folio ; Q. — quarto ; O. — octavo ; D. — duodecimo ; S. — sextodecimo ; M. — Mark or Marks, the Mark, as well as the Shilling (*s.*), being reckoned at 25 cents. *Prices* quoted in Marks *are for unbound books if the letter b. is not added.*

† The retail price is given and is subject in most cases to discount.

Harpers' Latin Dictionary. A New Latin Dictionary, Founded on the Translation of Freund's Latin-German Lexicon ; edited by E. A. Andrews. Revised, enlarged, and in great part rewritten by C. T. Lewis and Ch. Short. New York, Harper & Bros., 1884. Q. $6.00.

Lewis, C. T., A Latin Dictionary for Schools. New York, Harper & Bros., 1889. O. $5.50.

Lewis, C. T., An Elementary Latin Dictionary. New edition. New York, Harper & Bros., 1895. O. $2.00.

White, J. T., An English-Latin Dictionary. New edition. Boston, Ginn & Co., 1882. O. $1.65.

Meissner, C., Latin Phrase-Book ; translated from the 6th German edition, with addition of supplementary phrases and references by H. W. Auden. New York, Macmillan & Co., 1894. D. $1.10.

Merguet, H., Lexikon zu den Reden des Cicero mit Angabe sämmtlicher Stellen. Jena, Fischer, 1877-84. 4 volumes. O. 189 M.

Merguet, H., Lexikon zu den philosophischen Schriften Cicero's mit Angabe sämmtlicher Stellen. Jena, Fischer, 1887–94. 3 volumes. O. 136 M.

Meusel, H., Lexicon Caesarianum. Berlin, W. Weber, 1887–93. 2 volumes in 3. O. 45 M.

Boeckh, Aug., Encyclopädie und Methodologie der philologischen Wissenschaften ; herausgegeben von E. Bratuscheck. 2d edition, besorgt von R. Klussmann. Leipzig, B. G. Teubner, 1886. O. 14 M.

Reinach, S., Manuel de philologie classique. Paris, Librarie Hachette et Cie. Volume I., 2d edition, 1883 ; volume II., 1884. O. 15 Francs. ($3.00.)

Gudeman, A., Outlines of the History of Classical Philology. 2d edition. Boston, Ginn & Co., 1894. D. $1.05.

Hübner, E., Bibliographie der klassischen Alterthumswissenschaft. Grundriss zu Vorlesungen über die Geschichte und Encyclopädie der klassischen Philologie. 2d edition, enlarged. Berlin, Hertz, 1889. O. 15 M.

Engelmann, Wilh. (*editor*), Bibliotheca scriptorum classicorum. 8th edition, embracing the literature from 1700–1878, revised by E. Preuss. Leipzig, Wilh. Engelmann, 1880–82. 2 parts. O. 36 M.

Mayor, J. B., Guide to the Choice of Classical Books. 3d edition. London, George Bell & Sons, 1885. O. $1.25. A new supplement, 1879–1896, New York, The Macmillan Co., 1897. $1.25.

Adams C. K., A Manual of Historical Literature, comprising brief descriptions of the most important histories in English, French and German, together with practical suggestions as to methods and courses of historical study ; for the use of students, general readers and collectors of books. 3d edition, revised and enlarged. New York, Harper & Bros., 1889. O. $2.50.

The American Journal of Philology; edited by B. L. Gildersleeve (*published quarterly*). Baltimore, Friedenwald & Co., 1881—. $3.00 *per year.*

The American Journal of Archæology and of the History of the Fine Arts (*published quarterly*). Princeton University Press, 1885–96. $5.00 *per year. Back numbers for sale by* The Macmillan Co., New York, *who in 1897 began the publication of the continuation of this periodical, with the title:*

The American Journal of Archæology. Second series; edited by J. H. Wright, J. R. Wheeler, and A. Marquand (*published quarterly*). $5.00 *per year.*

The Classical Review (*published monthly*). London, David Nutt; Boston, Ginn & Co., 1887—. *$3.00 per year* (*9 Nos*).

Alaudæ (*Latin journal*). Aquila. Imported by L. Bohn, 351 East 52d St., New York. O. $ .60 *per year.*

Harper's Dictionary of Classical Literature and Antiquities; edited by H. T. Peck. Illustrated. New York, Harper & Bros., 1897. Q. $6.00.

Smith, Wm., Wayte, Wm., and Marindin, G. E. (*editors*), Dictionary of Greek and Roman Antiquities. 3d edition, revised and enlarged. Boston, Little, Brown and Co., 1890–1. 2 volumes. O. $14.00.

Seyffert, O., A Dictionary of Classical Antiquities, Mythology, Religion, Literature and Art; translated from the German. Revised and edited with additions by H. Nettleship and J. E. Sandys. New York, Macmillan & Co., 1891. O. $3.00.

Ramsay, W., A Manual of Roman Antiquities. 15th edition, revised and partly rewritten. New York, Charles Scribner's Sons, 1895. D. $3.00.

Rich, A., A Dictionary of Roman and Greek Antiquities. 3d edition, revised and improved. New York, Longmans, Green & Co., 1874. O. $2.50.

Gow, J., A Companion to School Classics. 3d edition, revised. New York, Macmillan & Co., 1893. D. $1.75.

Gardner, P., and Jevons, F. B., A Manual of Greek Antiquities. Illustrated. New York, Charles Scribner's Sons, 1895. D. $4.00.

Smith, Wm., Dictionary of Greek and Roman Geography. New edition. Boston, Little, Brown and Co., 1854–7. 2 volumes. O. $12.00.

Smith, Wm., Dictionary of Greek and Roman Biography and Mythology. Boston, Little, Brown & Co., 1844–9. 3 volumes. O. $18.00.

Guhl, E., and Koner, W., The Life of the Greeks and Romans, described from Antique Monuments; translated from the 3d German edition by F. Hueffer. New York, D. Appleton & Co., 1889. O. $2.50.

Becker, W. A., Gallus; or, Roman Scenes of the Time of Augustus, with Notes and Excursuses illustrative of the Manners and Customs of the Romans; translated by F. Metcalfe. 3d edition. New York, Longmans, Green & Co., 1882. O. $2.50.

Becker, W. A., Charicles—Illustrations of the Private Life of the Ancient Greeks, with Notes and Excursuses; translated from the German by F. Metcalfe. 3d edition. New York, Longmans, Green & Co., 1882. O. $2.50.

von Falke, J., Greece and Rome. Their Life and Art, translated [from the German] by Wm. H. Browne. New York, Henry Holt & Co. Old edition. F. 1885. $15.00. New edition, 1886. $10.00.

von Mueller, Iwan (*editor*), Handbuch der klassischen Altertumswissenschaft in systematischer Darstellung, mit besonderer Rücksicht auf Geschichte und Methodik der einzelnen Disciplinen. Munich, Beck'sche Buchhandlung. Large O.

> Vol. I. 2d edition. 1892. 17 M. b. Einleitende und Hülfs-Disciplinen. *Contents:* Grundlegung und Geschichte der Philologie by L. von Urlichs. Hermeneutik und Kritik, Fr. Blass. Palæographie, Buchwesen und Handschriftkunde, Fr. Blass. Griechische Epigraphik, G. Hinricks. Römische Epigraphik, E. Hübner. Zeitrechnung der Griechen und Römer, G. Fr. Unger. Griechische und römische Metrologie, H. Nissen.

Vol. II. 2d edition, 1890.   15.50 M. b.   Griechische und lateinische Sprachwissenschaft. *Contents:* Griechische Grammatik, K. Brugmann. Lateinische Grammatik, Fr. Stolz, J. H. Schmalz. Griechische Lexikographie, G. Autenrieth. Lateinische Lexikographie, F. Heerdegen. Rhe-
torik, R. Volkmann. Metrik der Griechen und Römer mit einem Anhang über die Musik der Griechen, H. Gleditsch.

Vol. III. 1–3. 1889.   18.50 M. b.   Geographie und politische Geschichte
des klassischen Altertums, mit einer Einleitung über die Geographie und
Geschichte des Orients bis zu den Perserkriegen. *Contents:* Abriss der
Geschichte der vorder asiatischen Kulturvölker und Ägyptens, Fr. Hom-
mel. Geographie und Geschichte des griechischen Altertums, H. G.
Lolling und R. Pöhlmann. Geographie und Geschichte des römischen
Altertums, J. Jung, B. Niese und O. Richter (Topographie von Rom).

Vol. III. 4. 2d edition, 1896.   6.50 M. b.   Grundriss der griechischen
Geschichte nebst Quellenkunde, R. Pöhlmann.

Vol. III. 5. 2d edition, 1896.   5 M.   Grundriss der römischen Geschichte
nebst Quellenkunde, B. Niese.

Vol. IV. 1. 2d edition. 1892–3.   11.50 M. b.   Die griechischen Staats
und Rechtsaltertümer, G. Busolt. Die griechischen Privataltertümer,
Iwan von Müller. Die griechischen Kriegsaltertümer, A. Bauer.

Vol. IV. 2. 2d edition. 1893.   9.80 M. b.   Die römischen Staats- und
Kriegsaltertümer, H. Schiller. Privataltertümer, M. Voigt.

Vol. V. 1. 2d edition. 1894.   7.20 M. b.   Geschichte der antiken Mathematik, Naturwissenschaft und wissenschaftlichen Erdkunde, S. Günther.
Geschichte der Philosophie im Altertum, W. Windelband.

Vol. V. 3. 1890. 8.20 M. b.   Die griechischen Sakralaltertümer, P. Stengel.
Das Bühnenwesen der Griechen und Römer, G. Oehmichen.

Vol. VI. 1895.   5.50 M. b.   Archæologie der Kunst nebst einem Anhang
über die antike Numismatik, K. Sittl. (*With Atlas, 66 plates, con-
taining 1,000 illustrations and costing* 11.50 M.)

Vol VII. 2d edition, enlarged. 1890.   15.20 M. b.   Geschichte der griechischen Litteratur (*to the time of Justinian*), W. Christ.

Vol. VIII. 1, 2. 1890.   7.20 M. b.   Geschichte der römischen Litteratur
(*to the time of Hadrian*), M. Schanz.

Vol. VIII. 3. 1896.   7.50 M.   Geschichte der römischen Litteratur (from
Hadrian, 117 A. D., to Constantine, 324 A. D.), M. Schanz.

Vol. IX. 1. 1891.   10.50 M. b.   Geschichte der byzantinischen Litteratur
(from Justinian to the fall of the Eastern Empire, 527–1453 A. D.), K.
Krumbacher. (*Other volumes to follow.*)

II.   COMPARATIVE PHILOLOGY, AND THE CLASSICAL LANGUAGES.

a. Comparative Philology.*

Paul, H., Principles of the History of Language ; translated from the second edition
of the original (*Principien der Sprachgeschichte, Halle, 1886*) by H. A.
Strong. New York, Macmillan & Co., 1889. O. $3.00.

For further references see Henry, V., Comparative Grammar of Greek and Latin, pp. xix.–
xxviii.

Whitney, W. D., Language and the Study of Language. Twelve Lectures on the Principles of Linguistic Science. 4th edition. New York, Charles Scribner's Sons, 1884. O. $2.50.

Whitney, W. D., Life and Growth of Language : An Outline of Linguistic Science. (International Scientific Series, volume 16.) 6th edition. New York, D. Appleton & Co., 1892. O. $1.50.

Whitney, W. D., Oriental and Linguistic Studies. 1st series. New York, Charles Scribner's Sons, 1873. O. $2.50.

Taylor, I., Words and Places : or, Etymological Illustrations of History, Ethnology, and Geography. 3d edition. New York, Macmillan & Co., 1873. D. $1.60.

Delbrueck, B., Introduction to the Study of Language. A Critical Survey of the History and Methods of Comparative Philology of the Indo-European Languages ; translated by E. Channing. Boston, Ginn & Co., 1882. O. $1.00.

Schrader, O., Prehistoric Antiquities of the Aryan People ; translated from the 2d German edition by F. B. Jevons. London, Charles Griffin & Co., 1890. O. 21s.

Brugmann, K., Elements of the Comparative Grammar of the Indo-Germanic Languages. A Concise Exposition of the History of Sanskrit, old Iranian (Avestic and old Persian), old Armenian, old Greek, Latin, Umbrian-Samnitic, old Irish, Gothic, old High German, Lithuanian and old Church Slavonic ; translated from the German, volume I, by J. Wright, volumes II-IV and Index by R. S. Conway and W. H. D. Rouse. New York, B. Westermann, 1888-1895. O. $17.50. (*The 1st half of the third volume of the German edition, " Vergleichende Syntax," by B. Delbrueck, is not yet translated.*)

Giles, P., A Short Manual of Comparative Philology for Classical Students, with Appendices on the Greek and Latin Dialects and Alphabets. New York, Macmillan & Co., 1895. O. $3.00.

b. Greek and Latin Languages.

Henry, V., A Short Comparative Grammar of Greek and Latin for Schools and Colleges ; authorized translation from the 2d French edition by R. T. Elliott, with an introductory note by Henry Nettleship. New York, Macmillan & Co., 1890. D. $1.90.

Mueller, L., Greek and Roman Versification ; translated by S. B. Platner. Boston, Allyn & Bacon, 1892. D. $ .75.

Schmidt, J. H. H., An Introduction to the Rhythmic and Metric of the Classical Languages (with rhythmical schemes and commentaries on the lyrical parts of the Medea and the Antigone); translated from the German by J. W. White. Boston, Ginn & Co., 1880. O. $2.50.

Weil, H., The Order of Words in the Ancient Languages compared with that of Modern Languages ; translated, with notes and additions, by Ch. W. Super. Boston, Ginn & Co., 1887. O. $1.25. (*3d French edition, Paris, 1879.*)

Taylor, I., The Alphabet : An Account of the Origin and Development of Letters. London, Kegan Paul, Trench, Trübner & Co., 1883. 2 volumes. O. 36s. (*Volume I. discusses the Greek and Latin Alphabets.*)

Thompson, E. M., Handbook of Greek and Latin Palæography. (International Scientific Series.) New York, D. Appleton & Co., 1893. O. $2.00.

Johnston, H. W., Latin Manuscripts. An Elementary Introduction to the Use of Critical Editions. Chicago, Scott, Foresman & Company, 1897. Q. $2.25.

Lindsay, W. M., An Introduction to Latin Textual Emendation: Based on the Text of Plautus. New York, The Macmillan Company, 1896. O. $1.00.

c. Greek Language.

Kühner, R., Ausführliche Grammatik der griechischen Sprache. Part I., 3d edition; in 2 volumes, revised by Fr. Blass. Volume II. 2d edition. Hannover, Hahn, 1886–92. O. 27 M.

Meyer, G., Griechische Grammatik. 2d edition. Leipzig, Breitkopf & Härtel, 1886. O. 11 M.

Goodwin, W. W., Syntax of the Moods and Tenses of the Greek Verb. Rewritten and enlarged. Boston, Ginn & Co., 1893. O. $2.15.

Seymour, T. D., Introduction to the Language and Verse of Homer. Boston, Ginn & Co., 1885. D. .80.

Monro, D. B., A Grammar of the Homeric Dialect. 2d edition, revised and enlarged. New York, Macmillan & Co., 1891. O. $3.50.

Blass, Fr., Pronunciation of Ancient Greek; translated from the 3d German edition by W. J. Purton. New York, Macmillan & Co., 1890. O. $1.90.

Veitch, Wm., Greek Verbs Irregular and Defective, their Forms, Meaning and Quantity. 4th edition. New York, Macmillan & Co., 1887. O. $2.50.

Roberts, E. S., An Introduction to Greek Epigraphy. Part I. The Archaic Inscriptions and the Greek Alphabet. New York, Macmillan & Co., 1887. O. $4.50.

Cauer, P. (*editor*), Delectus inscriptionum Græcarum propter dialectum memorabilium. 2d edition. Leipzig, S. Hirzel, 1883. O. 7 M.

Smyth, H. W., The Sounds and Inflections of the Greek Dialects. Volume I. Ionic. New York, Macmillan & Co., 1894. O. $6.00.

Kirchhoff, J. W. A., Studien zur Geschichte des griechischen Alphabets. 4th edition. Gütersloh, Bertelsmann, 1887. O. 6 M.

Rizo-Rangabé, E., A Practical Method in the Modern Greek Language. Boston, Ginn & Co., 1896. D. $2.00.

d. Latin Language.

Kühner, R., Ausführliche Grammatik der lateinischen Sprache. Hannover, Hahn, 1877–79. 2 volumes in 3. O. 25 M.

Roby, H. J., A Grammar of the Latin Language from Plautus to Suetonius. 5th edition. New York, Macmillan & Co., 1882-7. 2 volumes. D. $4.50.

Madvig, I. N., A Latin Grammar for the Use of Schools; translated with the sanction and coöperation of the author by G. Woods. 1st American edition from the 5th English edition by T. A. Thatcher. Boston, Ginn & Co., 1870. O. $2.40.

Gildersleeve, B. L., and Lodge, G., Gildersleeve's Latin Grammar. 3d edition, revised and enlarged. New York, University Publishing Co., 1894. O. $1.50.

Bennett, C. E., A Latin Grammar. 4th edition. Boston, Allyn & Bacon, 1896.

Also Appendix to Bennett's Latin Grammar. *Same publisher*, 1895 ; *both* D. 80c *each. Complete edition*, $1.25.

Hale, W. G., Syntax of the Latin Moods and Tenses. Boston, Ginn & Co. O. $1.50. (*In press.*)

Neue, Fr., Formenlehre der lateinischen Sprache. Berlin, S. Calvary & Co. Volume I. 2d edition. 1877; volumes II–III, 1–9. 3d edition gänzlich neu bearbeitet von C. Wagener, 1892—. O. Volume I, 24 M., Volume II, 32 M., Volume III, 1–9, 18 M. (*The remainder of Volume III. will soon be issued; Volume I is to be revised later.*)

Lindsay, W. M., The Latin Language. An Historical Account of Latin Sounds, Stems and Inflections. New York, Macmillan & Co., 1894. O. $5.00.

Hale, W. G., The *Cum*-constructions ; their History and Functions (*forms Volume I. of " Cornell Studies in Classical Philology"*). Boston, Ginn & Co., 1887–9. O. $1.20. *The same is translated into German by A. Neitzert, with a preface by B. Delbrueck, revised and supplemented by the author.* Leipzig, B. G. Teubner, 1891. O. 6 M..

Menge, H., Repetitorium der lateinischen Syntax und Stilistik. 6th edition. Wolfenbüttel, Zwissler, 1890.— O. 7 M.

Potts, A. W., Hints towards Latin Prose Composition. New edition. New York, Macmillan & Co., 1886. 75c.

Weise, F. O., Charakteristik der lateinischen Sprache. Ein Versuch. Leipzig, B. G. Teubner, 1891. O. 2.40 M.

Krebs, J. Ph., Antibarbarus der lateinischen Sprache, nebst einem kurzen Abriss der Geschichte der lateinischen Sprache und Vorbemerkungen über reine Latinität. Sechste Auflage in vollständiger Umarbeitung der von A. D. Allgayer besorgten fünften Ausgabe von J. H. Schmalz. Basel, Benno Schwabe, 1886–88. 2 volumes. O. 24 M. b.

Brambach, W., Aids to Latin Orthography, translated by W. G. McCabe. New York, Harper & Bros., 1877. S. $1.00.

Döderlein, L., Hand-book of Latin Synonyms ; translated by H. H. Arnold. With an introduction by S. H. Taylor. Andover, W. F. Draper, 1875. O. $1.25.

Allen, F. D., Remnants of Early Latin ; selected and explained for the use of students. Boston, Ginn & Co., 1884. D. $ .80.

Wordsworth, J., Fragments and Specimens of Early Latin. With introductions and notes. New York, Macmillan & Co., 1874. O. $4.50.

Egbert, J. E., Introduction to the Study of Latin Inscriptions. New York, American Book Co., 1896. O. $3.50.

Rushforth, G. McN., Latin Historical Inscriptions illustrating the History of the Early Empire. New York, Macmillan & Co., 1893. O. $3.00.

Wilmanns, G. (*editor*), Exempla inscriptionum Latinarum in usum præcipue academicum composuit. Berlin, Weidmann, 1873. 2 volumes. O. 20 M.

Dessau, H. (*editor*), Inscriptiones Latinæ selectæ. Berlin, Weidmann, 1892. O. Volume I. 11 M. (*Only one volume has been published.*)

III. *GREEK AND LATIN LITERATURE.*
a. Works of a General Character.

Butcher, S. H., Aristotle's Theory of Poetry and Fine Art. With a Critical Text and a Translation of the Poetics. New York, Macmillan & Co., 1895. O. $3.50.

Arnold, M., On Translating Homer.   In volume II. of his Complete Works.   New York, Macmillan & Co., 1893.   D. $1.50.

Moulton, R. G., The Ancient Classical Drama.   A Study in Literary Evolution intended for Readers in English and in the Original.   New York, Macmillan & Co., 1890.   O. $2.25.

von Schlegel, A. W., Lectures on Dramatic Art and Literature ; translated by John Black.   Revised according to the last German edition by A. J. W. Morrison.   New York, Macmillan & Co., 1879.   O. $1.00.

Church, A. J., Stories from 1) Homer, 2) Virgil, 3) Greek Tragedians, 4) Livy, 5) Herodotus, 6) Pliny, 7) Lucian.   New York, Dodd, Mead & Co.   O. $1.00 *each.*

b. Greek Literature.

A. GENERAL HISTORIES AND WORKS ON PARTICULAR AUTHORS AND SUBJECTS.

Mure, Wm., A Critical History of the Language and Literature of Antient Greece.   2d edition.   London, Longmans, Green & Co., 1853–57.   5 volumes.   O.   69s.

Müller, K. O., A History of the Literature of Ancient Greece, continued after the author's death by J. W. Donaldson.   New York, Longmans, Green & Co., 1850–58.   3 volumes.   O.   36s.

Mahaffy, J. P., A History of Classical Greek Literature, with an Appendix on Homer (*In Volume I.*) by Professor Sayce.   New York, Macmillan & Co., 1885.   2 volumes.   D. $2.25 *each.*

Jevons, F. B., A History of Greek Literature, from the Earliest Period to the Death of Demosthenes.   New York, Charles Scribner's Sons, 1886.   O. $2.50.

Jebb, R. C., Greek Literature.   New York, D. Appleton & Co., 1879.   S. $.35.

Ancient Classics for English Readers ; edited by W. L. Collins.   Philadelphia, J. B. Lippincott Co.   28 volumes in 9.   S. $6.75.   *The* Greek *authors treated are* :

> Homer's Iliad, Homer's Odyssey, Herodotus, Æschylus, Xenophon, Sophocles, Euripides, Aristophanes, Hesiod and Theognis, Greek Anthology, Plato, Lucian, Demosthenes, Aristotle, Thucydides, Pindar.   [*Each volume is also sold separately.*]

Jebb, R. C., Homer: An Introduction to the Iliad and the Odyssey.   2d edition.   Boston, Ginn & Co., 1887.   D. $1.25.

Clerke, Agnes M., Familiar Studies in Homer.   New York, Longmans, Green & Co., 1892.   O. $1.75.

Bonitz, H., The Origin of the Homeric Poems, a Lecture ; translated from the 4th German edition, by L. R. Packard.   New York, Harper & Bros., 1880.   S. $ .75.

Lang, A., Homer and the Epic.   New York, Longmans, Green & Co., 1893.   O. $2.25.

Campbell, L., A Guide to Greek Tragedy for English Readers.   New York, G. P. Putnam's Sons, 1891.   D. $1.50.

De Quincey, Thos., Theory of Greek Tragedy.   In volume X. of his Collected Writings ; edited by D. Masson.   New York, Macmillan & Co., 1890.   O. $1.25.   (*The same volume contains* " Greek Poets and Prose Writers Generally " *and* " The Greek Orators.")

Haigh, A. E., The Attic Theatre. A Description of the Stage and Theatre of the Athenians, and of the Dramatic Performances at Athens. New York, Macmillan & Co., 1889. O. $3.00.

Haigh, A. E., The Tragic Drama of the Greeks. New York, Macmillan & Co., 1896. Illustrated. O. $3.25.

Jebb, R. C., The Growth and Influence of Classical Greek Poetry. Lectures delivered in 1892 on the Percy Turnbull Memorial Foundation in the Johns Hopkins University. Boston, Houghton, Mifflin & Co., 1893. O. $1.50.

Symonds, J. A., Studies of the Greek Poets. 3d edition. New York, Macmillan & Co., 1893. 2 volumes. O. $6.00.

De Quincey, Thos., The Philosophy of Herodotus. In volume VI. of his Collected Writings, edited by D. Masson. New York, Macmillan & Co., 1889. O. $1.25.

Jebb, R. C., The Attic Orators from Antiphon to Isæos. 2d edition. New York, Macmillan & Co, 1890. Two volumes. O. $5.00.

Witt, C., The Retreat of the Ten Thousand ; translated from the German by Frances Younghusband, with a preface by H. G. Dakyns. New York, Longmans, Green & Co., 1891. D. $1.25.

B. EDITIONS AND TRANSLATIONS OF GREEK AUTHORS.

Homeri Ilias et Odyssea ; edidit W. Dindorf. Editio V. correctior quam curavit G. Henze. Leipzig, B. G. Teubner, 1883-85. 2 volumes. D. 3 M.

The Iliad ; edited with English notes and introduction by Walter Leaf. New York, Macmillan & Co., 1886-88. 2 volumes. O. $4.00 *each*.

Odyssey ; edited with English notes, appendices, etc., by W. W. Merry and the late James Riddell. Bks. I.–XII. 2d edition. New York, Macmillan & Co., 1886. O. $4.00.

Odyssey, Books XIII.–XXIV., with introduction, notes, etc., by W. W. Merry. 2d edition. New York, Macmillan & Co., 1882. D. $1.10.

Hymns. Die homerischen Hymnen ; herausgegeben und erläutert von A. Gemoll. Leipzig, B. G. Teubner, 1886. O. 6.80 M.

The Iliad and Odyssey ; translated by Wm. Cullen Bryant. Boston, Houghton, Mifflin & Co. 2 volumes. O. $5.00.

The Whole Works of Homer, the Prince of Poets in his Iliads and Odysseys ; translated according to the Greek by George Chapman. London, Chatto & Windus, 1875. O. 6s.

The Iliad of Homer ; done into English Prose by A. Lang, W. Leaf and Ernest Myers. New York, Macmillan & Co., 1883. D. $1.50.

The Odyssey of Homer, done into English Prose by S. H. Butcher and A. Lang. New York, Macmillan & Co., 1879. D. $1.50.

Homeric Hymns ; translated by Percy Bysshe Shelley. In the Globe edition of his works. New York, Macmillan & Co., 1890. O. $1.75.

The Homeric Hymns ; translated into English Prose by J. Edgar. Edinburgh, J. Thin, 1891. D. 3s. 6d.

Cyclic Poets. Epicorum Græcorum fragmenta. Collegit, disposuit, commentarium criticum adiecit G. Kinkel. Volume I. Leipzig, B. G. Teubner, 1877. D. 3 M.

Hesiod. The Epics of Hesiod with an English Commentary by F. A. Paley. 2d edition. New York, Macmillan & Co., 1883. O. $1.75.

Anthologia lyrica, sive Lyricorum Græcorum veterum præter Pindarum reliquiæ potiores; Post Th. Bergkium quartum edidit E. Hiller. Leipzig, B. G. Teubner, 1890. D. 3 M.

Æschylus. The Tragedies of Æschylus; re-edited with an English Commentary by F. A. Paley. 4th edition. New York, Macmillan & Co., 1879. O. $2.75.

The Tragedies of Æschylus; a new translation with a biographical essay, and an appendix of rhymed choral odes by E. H. Plumptre. New edition. Boston, D. C. Heath & Co., 1890. D. $1.25.

Sophocles; edited with English notes and introduction by L. Campbell. New York. Macmillan & Co. Volume I. 2d edition, 1872; volume II., 1881. $4.00 each.

The Tragedies of Sophocles; a new translation with a biographical essay and an appendix of rhymed choral odes and lyrical dialogues by the late E. H. Plumptre. Boston, D. C. Heath & Co., 1882. D. $1.25.

Pindar. The Nemean and Isthmian Odes; with notes, explanatory and critical, introduction and introductory essays, by C. A. M. Fennell. 1883. D. $2.50. The Olympian and Pythian Odes, by same editor. 2d edition. 1893. D. $2.25. New York, Macmillan & Co.

The Extant Odes of Pindar; translated into English, with an introd. and short notes by E. Myers. New York, Macmillan & Co., 1874. D. $1.50.

Aristophanis Comœdiæ; edidit Th. Bergk. Editio altera correctior. Leipzig, B. G. Teubner, 1872. 2 volumes. D. 3 M.

Theocrit's Gedichte; erklärt von H. Fritsche. 3d edition besorgt von E. Hiller. Leipzig, B. G. Teubner, 1881. O. 2.70 M.

Theocritus, Bion and Moschus; rendered into English prose with an introductory essay by A. Lang. New York, Macmillan & Co., 1880. D. $1.00.

Herodotus; with a Commentary by J. W. Blakesley. New York, Macmillan & Co., 1854. 2 volumes. O. $4.50.

The History of Herodotus; translated into English by G. C. Macaulay. New York, Macmillan & Co., 1890. 2 volumes. D. $4.50.

Thucydides. *In* Ginn & Co.'s College Series of Greek Authors (*incomplete*). Erklärt von J. Klassen. Berlin, Weidmann, volumes IV.–VIII., 2d edition, 1877, '82, '84, '85; volumes I. and II., 3d edition, 1879, 1892; volume III., 4th edition, 1892 (volumes II. and III., revised by J. Steupp.) 8 volumes. O. (*Steupp's revision will cost, when complete, about 20 M.*)

Thucydides; translated and annotated by B. Jowett. New York, Macmillan & Co., 1881. 2 volumes. O. $8.00.

Xenophontis Historia Graeca; recensuit O. Keller. Editio minor. Leipzig, B. G. Teubner, 1889. D. .90 M.

* Xenophontis Expeditio Cyri; recensuit A. Hug. Editio minor. Leipzig, B. G. Teubner, 1878. D. .75 M.

Xenophontis Institutio Cyri; recensuit et præfatus est A. Hug. Editio minor. Leipzig, B. G. Teubner, 1883. D. .90 M.

Xenophontis Scripta minora; recognovit L. Dindorf. 2d edition corrected. Leipzig, B. G. Teubner, 1873. D. .90 M.

For references to the editions and literature of the Anabasis see Xenophon's Anabasis, Books I.–IV., edited by Francis W. Kelsey and Andrew C. Zenos, fourth edition, pp. 393–396. Boston, Allyn and Bacon, 1895.

The Works of **Xenophon**; translated by H. G. Dakyns. New York, Macmillan & Co. 4 volumes. D. Volume I., 1890; II., 1892. $5.00. Volumes III. *and* IV. *not yet published.*

Platonis Dialogi secundum Thrasylli tetralogias dispositi; post C. F. Hermann recognovit M. Wohlrab. [*Volumes I. and II. only revised by* Wohlrab.] Leipzig, B. G. Teubner, 1873–89. 6 volumes. O. 9.75 M.

*The Dialogues of Plato; translated into English with Analyses and Introductions by B. Jowett. 3d edition, revised. New York, Macmillan & Co., 1892. 5 volumes. O. $20.00.

Euripides; with an English commentary by F. A. Paley. 2d edition, revised and corrected. London, Whittaker & Co., 1872–80. 3 volumes. O. 8s. *each.*

The Tragedies of Euripides in English Verse; by A. S. Way. New York, Macmillan & Co., Volume I., 1894; Volume II., 1896. D. $2.00 *each.* (Volume III. *not yet published.*)

O R A T O R E S A T T I C I :

Antiphontis Orationes et fragmenta adiunctis Gorgiæ, Antisthenis, Alcidamantis declamationibus; edidit Fr. Blass. Editio altera correctior. Leipzig, B. G. Teubner, 1881. D. 2.10 M.

Andocidis Orationes; edidit Fr. Blass. Leipzig, B. G. Teubner, 1880. D. 1.20 M.

Lysiæ Orationes; ad codicum Palatinum nunc denuo collatum recensuit C. Scheibe. Accedunt orationum deperditarum fragmenta. 2d edition, revised and enlarged. Leipzig, B. G. Teubner, 1876. D. 1.20 M.

Isocratis Orationes; recognovit, præfatus est, indicem nominum addidit G. E. Benseler. 2d edition by Fr. Blass. Leipzig, B. G. Teubner, 1878–9. 2 volumes. D. 2.70 M.

Isæi Orationes cum aliquot deperditarum fragmentis; edidit C. Scheibe. Leipzig, B. G. Teubner, 1894. D. 1.20 M.

Demosthenis Orationes; ex recensione W. Dindorf. Editio quarta correctior curante Fr. Blass. 4th edition. Leipzig, B. G. Teubner, 1885–89. 3 volumes. D. 7.20 M.

Æschinis Orationes; post Fr. Franke curavit Fr. Blass. Leipzig, B. G. Teubner, 1896. D. 2.40 M.

Lycurgi Oratio in Leocratem; edidit C. Scheibe. Leipzig, B. G. Teubner, 1871. D. .60 M.

Hyperidis Orationes quattuor cum ceterarum fragmentis; edidit Fr. Blass. 2d edition. Leipzig, B. G. Teubner, 1881. D. 1.35 M.

Dinarchi Orationes adiunctis **Demadis** qui fertur fragmentis ὑπὲρ τῆς δωδεκαετίας; edidit Fr. Blass. 2d edition. Leipzig, B. G. Teubner, 1888. D. 1.00 M.

Aristotelis Opera omnia; Græce et Latine cum indice rerum et nominum absolutissimo. Paris, Firman Didot, 1848–74. 5 volumes. O. 80 Francs. ($16.00.)

The Politics of Aristotle; translated with notes by J. E. C. Welldon. New York, Macmillan & Co., 1888. O. $2.50.

As a partial substitute may be purchased: A Selection from Plato for English Readers, from the Translation by B. Jowett; edited with an introduction by M. J. Knight. New York, Macmillan & Co., 1895. 2 volumes. O. $5.00.

The Nicomachean Ethics of Aristotle ; . translated with an analysis and critical notes by J. E. C. Welldon. New York, Macmillan & Co., 1892. O. $2.00.

The Rhetoric of Aristotle ; translated with notes by J. E. C. Welldon. New York, Macmillan & Co., 1886. O. $2.00.

Aristotle's Constitution of Athens. A Revised Text with an Introduction, Critical and Explanatory Notes, Testimonia, Indices, by J. E. Sandys. New York, Macmillan & Co., 1893. O. $3.75.

Polybii Historiæ; recensuit, apparatu critico instruxit Fr. Hultsch. 2d edition. Berlin, Weidmann, 1870-92. 4 volumes. D. 16.50 M.

Dionysi Halicarnasensis Antiquitatum Romanarum quae supersunt ; edidit C. Jacoby. Leipzig, B. G. Teubner, 1885—. Volumes I.-III. D. 9.60 M. Volume IV. *in Press.*

Diodori [Siculi] Bibliotheca historica. Editionem primam curavit I. Bekker, alteram L. Dindorf. Recognovit F. Vogel. Leipzig, B. G. Teubner, 1867-93. 5 volumes. D. Volumes I.-III., 11.20 M.; Volumes IV.-V. (*not yet revised by Vogel*), 5.40 M.

Longinus, On the Sublime ; translated into English by H. L. Havell. With an introduction by A. Lang. New York, Macmillan & Co., 1890. O. $1.10.

Plutarchi Vitæ parallelæ ; iterum recognovit C. Sintenis. Leipzig, B. G. Teubner, 1873-74. 5 volumes. D. 8.40 M.

Moralia ; recognovit G. N. Bernardakis. Leipzig, B. G. Teubner, 1888-95. 6 volumes. D. 19 M.

Plutarch's Lives. Partly from Dryden's translation and partly from other hands ; the whole carefully revised and corrected, with some original translation by the editor, A. H. Clough. Boston, Little, Brown & Co., 1888. O. $2.00.

Morals ; translated from the Greek by several hands, corrected and revised by Wm. W. Goodwin. With an introduction by Ralph Waldo Emerson. Boston, Little, Brown & Co., 1871. 5 volumes. O. $15.00.

Strabonis Geographica ; recognovit A. Meineke. Leipzig, B. G. Teubner, 1866. 3 volumes. 6 M.

Flavius Josephus, The Works of. Whiston's translation ; revised by A. R. Shilleto, with topographical notes by C. W. Wilson. New York, Macmillan & Co., 1889-90. 5 volumes. D. $5.00.

Dionis Cassii Cocceiani Historia Romana. Editionem primam curavit L. Dindorf. Recognovit J. Melber. Leipzig, B. G. Teubner. Volume I., 1890, Volume II., 1894. D. 8.60 M. Volumes III.-V. *not yet revised ; old edition of volumes* III.-V., 1864-65. D. 8.10 M.

The New Testament in the Original Greek ; the text revised by B. F. Westcott and F. J. A. Hort. New York, Macmillan & Co., 1882, 1890. 2 volumes. D. $4.00.

Epictetus, The Discourses of, with the Encheiridion and Fragments ; translated with notes, a life of Epictetus, a view of his philosophy, and index, by Geo. Long. New York, Macmillan & Co., 1877. $1.50. [*Fine paper edition,* 2 volumes, $3.00.]

Pausaniae Descriptio Græciæ , recognovit J. H. Schubart. Leipzig, B. G. Teubner, 1875. 2 volumes. D. 3.60 M.

Pausanias' Description of Greece ; translated with notes and index by A. R. Shilleto. New York, Macmillan & Co., 1886. 2 volumes. O. $1.50 *each.*

Pausanias' Description of Greece ; translated with a commentary by J. G. Frazer. New York, The Macmillan Co., 1897. 6 volumes. O. $25.00.

Arriani Nicomediensis Scripta minora ; R. Hercher iterum recognovit ; edenda curavit A. Eberhard. Leipzig, B. G. Teubner, 1885. D. 1.00 M. Arriani Anabasis ; recognovit C. Abicht. Leipzig, B. G. Teubner, 1876. D. 1.20 M.

Arrian. Anabasis of Alexander and Indica ; translated with copious commentary by E. J. Chinnock. New York, Macmillan & Co., 1893. O. $1.50.

Lucianus; recognovit J. Sommerbrodt. Berlin, Weidmann. Volumes I. and II., 1886-96. O. 20.40 M.

Marcus Aurelius. The Thoughts of the Emperor Marcus Aurelius Antoninus ; translated by Geo. Long. 7th edition. Boston, Little, Brown & Co., 1889. O. $1.50.

Diogenes Laërtius ; translated by C. D. Yonge. New York, Macmillan & Co. 1853. D. $1.50.

b. *Latin Literature.*

A. GENERAL HISTORIES AND WORKS ON PARTICULAR AUTHORS AND SUBJECTS.

Teuffel, W. S., History of Roman Literature ; revised and enlarged by Ludwig Schwabe. Authorized translation from the 5th German edition by G. C. W. Warr. New York, Macmillan & Co., 1891-92. 2 volumes. O. $4.00 *each.*

Middleton, G., and **Mills, T. R.,** The Student's Companion to Latin Authors. New York, The Macmillan Co., 1896. O. $1.50.

Cruttwell, C. T., A History of Roman Literature from the Earliest Period to the Death of Marcus Aurelius. 2d edition. New York, Charles Scribner's Sons, 1888. O. $2.50.

Dunlop, John, History of Roman Literature from its Earliest Period to the Augustan Age (2 volumes, 1824. 2d edition) and during the Augustan Age (1 volume, 1828). New York, Longmans, Green & Co. O.

Bender, H., A Brief History of Roman Literature for Schools and Colleges ; translated and edited from the German by E. P. Crowell and H. B. Richardson. 2d edition. Boston, Ginn & Co., 1880. D. $1.00.

Kelsey, F. W., Topical Outline of Latin Literature; with References. Boston, Allyn & Bacon, 1891. D. $ .35. [*Bibliographical.*]

Harrington, K. P., Helps to the Intelligent Study of College Preparatory Latin. Boston, Ginn & Co., 1888. D. $ .35. [*Bibliographical.*]

Ancient Classics for English Readers ; edited by W. L. Collins. Philadelphia, J. B. Lippincott Co., 28 volumes in 9. S. $6.75. *The* Roman *authors treated are :* Cæsar, Virgil, Horace, Cicero, Pliny's Letters, Juvenal, Plautus and Terence, Tacitus, Livy, Ovid, Catullus, Lucretius. [*Each volume is also sold separately.*]

Tyrrell, R. Y., Latin Poetry, Lectures delivered in 1893 on the Percy Turnbull Memorial Foundation in the Johns Hopkins University. Boston, Houghton, Mifflin & Co., 1895. O. $1.50.

Sellar, W. Y., The Roman Poets of the Republic. 3d edition enlarged. New York, Macmillan & Co., 1889. O. $2.50.

Newman, J. H., Marcus Tullius Cicero. In volume II. of his Historical Sketches. New York, Longmans, Green and Co., 1891. O. $1.25.

Forsyth, Wm., Life of Marcus Tullius Cicero. 2d American edition. New York, Charles Scribner's Sons, 1865. 2 volumes. O. $2.50.

Faussett, W. Y., The Student's Cicero; adapted from the German of Dr. Munk's Geschichte der römischen Literatur. New York, Macmillan & Co., 1890. D. $1.00.

De Quincey, Thos., Cicero. In volume VI. of Collected Writings, edited by D. Masson. New York, Macmillan & Co., 1890. D. $1.25.

Trollope, A., The Life of Cicero. New York, Harper & Bros, 1880. 2 volumes. O. $3.00.

Dodge, T. A., Cæsar. A History of the Art of War among the Romans down to the End of the Roman Empire, with a Detailed Account of the Campaigns of Caius Julius Cæsar. Boston, Houghton, Mifflin & Co., 1892. O. $5.00.

Froude, J. A., Cæsar : A Sketch. New York, Charles Scribner's Sons, 1879. O. $1.50.

Napoleon III., History of Julius Cæsar; translated. New York, Harper & Bros., 1865–66. 2 volumes and Atlas. O. $7.00. *Cheap edition*, $4.00.

von Goeler, A., Cæsars Gallischer Krieg und Theile seines Bürgerkrieges nebst Anhängen über das römische Kriegswesen und über römische Daten. Freiburg, J. C. B. Mohr, 1886. 2d edition. O. 18 M.

Heynacher, M., Was ergiebt sich aus dem Sprachgebrauch Cæsars im Bellum Gallicum für die Behandlung der lateinischen Syntax in der Schule. 2d edition enlarged. Berlin, Weidmann, 1886. D. 3 M.

Lupus, B., Der Sprachgebrauch des Cornelius Nepos. Berlin, Weidmann, 1876. O. 6.40 M.

Sellar, W. Y., The Roman Poets of the Augustan Age : Virgil. 2d edition. New York, Macmillan & Co., 1883. O. $2.25.

Nettleship, H., Ancient Lives of Vergil, with an essay on the poems of Vergil in connection with his life and times. New York, Macmillan & Co., 1879. O. $ .50.

Comparetti, D., Vergil in the Middle Ages ; translated by E. F. M. Benecke. With an introduction by R. Ellis. New York, Macmillan & Co., 1895. D. $2.25.

Sellar, W. Y., The Roman Poets of the Augustan Age : Horace and the Elegiac Group, with a memoir of the author by Andrew Lang. New York, Macmillan & Co., 1892. O. $3.50.

Conington, J., Miscellaneous Writings ; edited by J. A. Symonds. With a memoir by H. J. S. Smith. Vol. I., London, Longmans, Green & Co., 1872. O. 14s.

Nettleship, H., Lectures and Essays on Subjects connected with Latin Literature and Scholarship. New York, Macmillan & Co., 1885. O. $1.90.

B. EDITIONS AND TRANSLATIONS OF LATIN AUTHORS.

T. Macci Plauti Comœdiæ ; ex recensione G. Goetz et Fr. Schoell. Leipzig, B. G. Teubner, 1893–5. 7 parts. D. 9.70 M.

* P. Terenti Afri Comœdiæ ; recensuit C. Dziatzko. Leipzig, B. Tauchnitz, 1884. O. 1.20 M.

---

* For a full bibliography of Terence from the date of Dziatzko's edition, see P. Terenti Phormio with Notes and Introductions by H. C. Elmer, pp. 171-182. Boston, Leach, Shewell and Sanborn, 1895. D.

M. Porci Catonis De agri cultura liber; recognovit H. Keil. Leipzig, B. G. Teubner, 1895. D. 1.00 M.

M. Terenti Varronis Rerum rusticarum libri III; recognovit H. Keil. Leipzig, B. G. Teubner, 1889. D. 1.50 M.

*__Marci Tulli Ciceronis,__ Opera quae supersunt omnia; edidit J. G. Baiter et C. L. Kayser. Leipzig, B. Tauchnitz, 1860–9. 11 vols. O. 21.75 M.

The Correspondence of Marcus Tullius Cicero, arranged according to its Chronological Order; with a revision of the text, a commentary and introductory essays by R. Y. Tyrrell and L. C. Purser. New York, Macmillan & Co., 1879–94. 4 vols. O. $15.65. (*Not yet complete.*)

Orationes; With a Commentary by George Long. Volumes II.–IV., 1st edition; Volume I., 2d edition. New York, Macmillan & Co., 1855–62. O. Volumes I. and II., $5.50; Volumes III. and IV., *out of print.*

Marci Tullii Ciceronis De natura deorum libri tres; with introduction and commentary by J. B. Mayor, together with a new collation of several of of the English MSS. by J. H. Swainson. New York, Macmillan & Co., 1880, '83, '85. 3 volumes. O. $8.50.

M. Tulli Ciceronis Academica. The Text revised and explained [*with an Introduction on the Philosophy of Cicero*] by J. S. Ried. New York, Macmillan & Co., 1885. O. $3.75.

M. Tullii Ciceronis De oratore libri tres; with introduction and notes by A. C. Wilkins. Books I. and II., 2d edition; Book III., 1st edition. New York, Macmillan & Co., 1879–95. O. $4.50.

Cornelii Nepotis Vitæ; post C. Halm recognovit A. Fleckeisen. Leipzig, B. G. Teubner, 1884. D. .30 M.

† **C. Iulii Cæsaris** Commentarii cum Hirtii aliorumque supplementis; ex recensione Bernh. Kübler. Leipzig, B. G. Teubner, 1893–4. 2 vols. O. 2.10 M.

C. Julii Cæsaris Belli Gallici libri VII. A. Hirtii liber VIII.; recensuit, apparatu critico instruxit H. Meusel. Berlin, Weber, 1894. O. 4 M. b.

T. Lucreti Cari De rerum natura libri VI; with notes and a translation by H. A. J. Munro. 4th edition, finally revised. New York, Macmillan & Co., 1886. 3 volumes. O. Volumes I. and II., $4.50; volume III. (*translation*) $1.50.

C. Sallusti Crispi Catilina, Jugurtha, Historiarum reliquiæ codicibus servatæ. Accedunt rhetorum opuscula Sallustiana; H. Jordan tertium recognovit. 3d edition. Berlin, Weidmann, 1887. O. 1.50 M.

Catullus; edited by E. T. Merrill. (College Series of Latin Authors.) Boston, Ginn & Co., 1893. D. $1.50.

P. Vergili Maronis Opera. The Works of Virgil with a Commentary. Volumes I. and II. by J. Conington; Vol. III., 2d edition by J. Conington and H. Nettleship. New York, Macmillan & Co., 1872–1876. O. $9.75.

P. Vergili Maronis Opera. Virgil; with an Introduction and Notes by T. L.

Papillon and A. E. Haigh. New York, Macmillan & Co., 1892. O.
$2.75.

Publius Virgilius Maro varietate lectionis et perpetua adnotatione illustratus
a Christ. Gottl. Heyne. Editio quarta, curavit Ge. Phil. Eb. Wagner.
Leipzig and London, 1830–41. 5 volumes. O. 60 M.

Works of Virgil; translated by John Dryden. In the "Works of John Dryden." Globe edition, New York, Macmillan & Co. $1.75.

Poems; translated into English Prose by J. Conington. In volume II. of his
Miscellaneous Writings; edited by J. A. Symonds. London, Longmans,
Green & Co., 1872. 14s.

Q. Horatii Flacci Opera omnia; with a Commentary by E. C. Wickham. New York,
Macmillan & Co., Volume I., 2d edition, 1877; Volume II., 1891. O. $6.00.

Albii Tibulli Elegiæ cum carminibus pseudotibullianis; edidit E. Hiller. Accedit
index verborum. Leipzig, B. Tauchnitz, 1885. O. .60 M.

Sex. Properti Elegiarum libri IV.; recensuit A. Palmer. New York, Macmillan &
Co., 1880. O. $1.25.

*P. Ovidii Nasonis Carmina; edidit A. Riese. Leipzig, B. Tauchnitz, 1871–4. 3
volumes. O. 2.90 M.

T. Livi Ab urbe condita libri. Editionem primam curavit Wilh. Weissenborn.
Editio altera quam curavit M. Müller. Leipzig, B. G. Teubner. 6 vols. D.
6 M. Volumes II–IV only are revised by Müller.

Livi, Books I–X. With introduction, historical examination and notes by
J. R. Seeley. 3d edition. [Book I. alone has been published; valuable
for its historical introduction.] New York, Macmillan & Co., 1881.
O. $1.50.

Justini Epitoma historiarum Philippicarum Pompei Trogi; ex recensione F. Ruehl.
Accedunt prologi in Pompeium Trogum ab. A. de Gutschmid recensiti. Leipzig, B. G. Teubner, 1886. D. 1.50 M.

Annaei Senecae Oratorum et Rhetorum divisiones, colores, sententiae; recognovit A.
Kiessling. Leipzig, B. G. Teubner, 1872. D. 4.50 M.

M. Vellei Paterculi Ex historiæ Romanæ libris duobus quæ supersunt; apparatu
critico adiecto edidit C. Halm. Leipzig, B. G. Teubner, 1876. D. 1.00 M.

Valerii Maximi Factorum et dictorum memorabilium libri novem, cum Julii Paridis
et Ianuarii Nepotiani epitomis; iterum recensuit C. Kempf. Leipzig, B. G.
Teubner, 1888. D. 4.50 M.

Phædri Fabulae. Für Schüler mit Anmerkungen versehen von G. Siebelis. 6th corrected edition by Fr. Polle. Leipzig, B. G. Teubner, 1889. D. .75 M.

L. Annaei Senecæ Opera quæ supersunt; recognovit et indicem locupletissimum
adiecit Fr. Haase. Leipzig, B. G. Teubner, 1874, 1877, 1878. 3 volumes.
D. 7.80 M.

Tragœdiæ; recensuit et emendavit Fr. Leo. Berlin, Weidmann, 1878, 1879.
2 volumes. O. 9 M.

Q. Curtii Rufi Historiarum Alexandri Magni Macedonis qui supersunt; recognovit
Th. Vogel. Leipzig, B. G. Teubner, 1880. D. 1.20 M.

Persius. The Satires of Aulus Persius Flaccus, with a translation and commentary

---

* For further references to editions and books on the works of Ovid usually read in
secondary schools see Kelsey's Selections from Ovid, fourth edition, pp. 295-298. Boston, Allyn &
Bacon, 1897.

by J. Conington; edited by H. Nettleship.   3d edition, revised.   New York,
Macmillan & Co., 1893.   O. $2.25.

M. Annaei Lucani De bello civili libri X; G. Steinharti aliorumque copiis usus edidit
C. Hose.   Leipzig, B. G. Teubner, 1892.   D.   3.60 M.

C. Plini Secundi Naturalis historiæ libri XXXVII; edidit L. Jahn.   (*Revised in
part by* C. Mayhoff.)   Leipzig, B. G. Teubner, 1858–92.   6 vols.   D.
14.40 M.

C. Valeri Flacci Balbi Setini Argonauticon libri VIII; recognovit E. Baehrens.
Leipzig, B. G. Teubner, 1875.   D.   1.50 M.

P. Papinius Statius; volume I, Silvæ, recensuit E. Baehrens; volume II, Achil-
leis, Thebais, recensuit P. Kohlmann.   Leipzig, B. G. Teubner, 1876–84.   D.
7.35 M.

Sili Italici Punica; edidit L. Bauer.   Leipzig, B. G. Teubner, 1890–92.   2 volumes.   D.   4.80 M.

M. Valerii Martialis Epigrammaton libri; recognovit W. Gilbert.   Leipzig, B. G.
Teubner, 1886.   D.   2.40 M.

M. Fabi Quintiliani Institutionis oratoriæ libri I–XII; edidit Ferd. Meister.   Prag,
Tempski; Leipzig, Freytag; 1887.   2 volumes.   O.   2.70 M.

M. Fabi Quintiliani Declamationes quæ supersunt CXLV; recensuit C. Ritter.
Leipzig, B. G. Teubner, 1884.   D.   4.80 M.

Juvenal, Thirteen Satires, with a commentary by J. E. B. Mayor.   4th edition, revised.   New York, Macmillan & Co., 1888–9.   2 volumes.   D. $5.20.

Tacitus, Libri qui supersunt; quartum recognovit C. Halm.   4th edition.   Leipzig,
B. G. Teubner, 1883.   D.   2.40 M.

The Annals of Tacitus; edited with introduction and notes by H. Furneaux.
Volume I., 2d edition, 1896; volume II., 1st edition, 1891.   New York,
Macmillan & Co.   O. $9.50.

The Histories of Tacitus; with introduction, notes and an index by W. A.
Spooner.   New York, Macmillan & Co., 1891.   O. $3.50.

P. Corneli Taciti Dialogus de oratoribus; with prolegomena, critical apparatus,
exegetical and critical notes, bibliography and indices by A. Gudeman.
Boston, Ginn & Co., 1894. $3.00.

C. Plini Cæcili Secundi Epistularum libri IX, Epistularum ad Traianum liber,
Panegyricus; recognovit H. Keil.   Leipzig, B. G. Teubner, 1873.   D.   1.20 M.

C. Suetoni Tranquilli quæ supersunt omnia; recensuit C. L. Roth.   Leipzig, B. G.
Teubner, 1875.   D.   1.50 M.

A. Gellii Noctium Atticarum libri XX; ex recensione M. Hertz.   2d edition.
Leipzig, B. G. Teubner, 1886.   2 volumes.   4.20 M.

L. Annæi Flori Epitomæ libri II et **P. Annii Flori** fragmentum de Vergilio oratore
an pœta; edidit O. Rossbach.   Leipzig, B. G. Teubner, 1896.   D.   2.80 M.

M. Corneli Frontonis et Marci Aureli Imperatoris epistulæ, L. Veri et T. Antonini
Pii et Appiani epistularum reliquiæ; post Angelum Maium cum codicibus Am-
brosiano et Vaticano iterum contulit G. N. du Rieu.   Recensuit S. A. Naber.
Leipzig, B. G. Teubner, 1867.   D.   8 M.

Eutropi Breviarium ab urbe condita; recognovit F. Ruehl.   Leipzig, B. G. Teubner,
1887.   D.   .45 M.

Servii Grammatici qui feruntur in Vergilii carmina commentarii recensuit G. Thilo.
Leipzig, B. G. Teubner, 1881–87.   3 volumes.   O.   54.40 M.

Macrobius; Fr. Eyssenhardt iterum recognovit. Adiectæ sunt tabulæ. Leipzig, B. G. Teubner, 1893. D. 6 M.

Scriptores Historiæ Augustæ; iterum recensuit adparatumque criticum adidit H. Peter. Leipzig, B. G. Teubner, 1884. 2 volumes. D. 7.50 M.

Poetæ Latini Minores; recensuit et emendavit E. Bæhrens. Leipzig, B. G. Teubner, 1879–83. 5 volumes. D. 15.90 M.

Historicorum Romanorum Fragmenta ; collegit, disposuit, recensuit H. Peter. Leipzig, B. G. Teubner, 1883. D. 4.50 M.

IV. RELIGION AND MYTHOLOGY.

Roscher, W. H. (*editor*), Ausführliches Lexicon der griechischen und römischen Mythologie. Leipzig, B. G. Teubner, 1884—. O. 66 + M. (*Now in course of publication ; 33 parts have thus far been issued, extending to the letter M.*)

Lang, A., Myth, Ritual and Religion. New York, Longmans, Green & Co., 1887. 2 volumes. O. $7.00.

Fiske, John, Myths and Myth-makers. Old Tales and Superstitions interpreted by Comparative Mythology. Boston, Houghton, Mifflin & Co., 1874. O. $2.00.

Frazer, T. G., The Golden Bough : A Study in Comparative Religion. New York, Macmillan & Co., 1890. 2 volumes. O. $5.00.

Murray, A. S., Manual of Mythology : Greek and Roman, Norse and Old German, Hindoo and Egyptian Mythology. Reprinted from the 2d revised London edition. New York, Charles Scribner's Sons, 1888. O. $1.75.

Collignon, M., Manual of Mythology, in Relation to Greek Art ; translated and enlarged by Jane E. Harrison. London, H. Grevel & Co., 1890. O. 10s. 6d.

Gayley, C. M. (*editor*), Classic Myths in English Literature, based chiefly on Bulfinch's " Age of Fable " (1855), accompanied by an interpretative and illustrative commentary. 2d edition. Boston, Ginn & Co., 1895. O. $1.65.

Kingsley, C., The Heroes ; or Greek Fairy Tales for my Children. Revised edition. London, Macmillan & Co., 1888. O. $1.25.

de Coulanges, Fustel, The Ancient City : a Study on the Religion, Laws and Institutions of Greece and Rome ; translated from the latest French edition by W. Small. 3d edition. Boston, Lee & Shepherd, 1877. D. $1.60.

Dyer, L., Studies of the Gods in Greece at Certain Sanctuaries recently excavated. Being eight lectures given in 1890 at the Lowell Institute. New edition. New York, Macmillan & Co., 1894. D. $2.00.

V. PUBLIC AFFAIRS.

a. Geography.

Freeman, E. A., The Historical Geography of Europe. New York, Longmans, Green & Co., 1881. 2 volumes. O. $10.50.

Tozer, H. F., Classical Geography. New York, D. Appleton & Co., 1877. S. $.35.

Desjardins, E., Géographie historique et administrative de la Gaule romaine. [*With 59 plates, chiefly colored, and 93 woodcuts.*] Paris, Librairie Hachette et Cie., 1876–93. 4 volumes. Q. 78 Francs. ($15.60.)

Mahaffy, J. P., Greek Pictures drawn with Pen and Pencil. New York, F. H. Revell & Co., 1890. F. $3.20. (*See also Sec. VII. b.*)

Freeman, E. A., Studies of Travel. Volume I., Greece ; Volume II., Italy. New York, G. P. Putnam's Sons, 1893. D. $1.50.

b. *History and Chronology.*

Freeman, E. A., The Methods of Historical Study. Eight lectures read in the University of Oxford in Michaelmas Term, 1884. With an Inaugural Lecture on the Office of the Historical Professor. New York, Macmillan & Co., 1886. O. $2.50.

Creasy, Edw., The Fifteen Decisive Battles of the World : from Marathon to Waterloo. New York, Harper Bros. & Co., 1872. O. $1.00.

A. EASTERN.

Myers, P. V. N., The Eastern Nations and Greece. (Part I. of "Ancient History for Colleges and High Schools ;" edited by W. F. Allen and P. V. N. Myers.) Boston, Ginn & Co., 1889. D. $1.00.

Putnam's "Stories of the Nations" Series. New York, G. P. Putnam's Sons.
The following volumes at $1.50 *per volume :*
The Story of Persia. By S. G. W. Benjamin.
The Story of Phœnicia. By Geo. Rawlinson.
The Story of the Jews under Rome. By W. Douglas.
The Story of Ancient Egypt. By Geo. Rawlinson.

B. GREECE.

[*For legendary history see also under* Homer *in Class III. b.*]
"Stories of the Nations." *The following volumes :*
The Story of Alexander's Empire. By J. P. Mahaffy and A. Gilman.
The Story of Sicily. By E. A. Freeman.
The Story of the Byzantine Empire. By C. W. C. Oman.

Grote, Geo., History of Greece. Boston, Little, Brown & Co., 1888. 10 volumes. O. $17.50.

Curtius, E., The History of Greece ; translated by A. Wm. Ward. Revised after the last German edition by W. A. Packard. New York, Charles Scribner's Sons, 1888. 5 volumes. O. $10.00.

Duruy, V., History of Greece and of the Greek People to 146 B. C.; translated from the French. London, Kegan Paul, Trench, Trübner & Co., 1891. 8 volumes. O. £8 8s.

Holm, A., The History of Greece from its Commencement to the Close of the Independence of the Greek Nation. New York, Macmillan & Co., 1894–96. *Volumes I.–III. now ready.* O. $7.50.

Tsountas and Manatt, The Mycenaean Age. *See under Sec. VII., a,* " Histories of the Arts."

Oman, C. W. C., A History of Greece from the Earliest Times to the Macedonian Conquest. New York, Longmans, Green & Co., 1892. D. $1.50.

Cox, G. W., The Greeks and the Persians. 5th edition. (*In the* " Epochs of Ancient History" Series.) New York, Charles Scribner's Sons, 1886. D. $1.00.

Lloyd, W. W., The Age of Pericles. A History of the Politics and Arts of Greece from the Persian to the Peloponnesian War. New York, Macmillan & Co., 1875. 2 volumes. $8.00.

Cox, G. W., The Athenian Empire. 5th edition. (*In the* " Epochs of Ancient History" Series.) New York, Charles Scribner's Sons, 1887. D. $1.00.

Sankey, C., The Spartan and Theban Supremacies. 3d edition. (*In the* " Epochs

of Ancient History " Series.)   New York, Charles Scribner's Sons, 1884. D.
$1.00.

Dodge, T. A., Alexander.   A History of the Origin and Growth of the Art of War
from the Earliest Times to the Battle of Ipsus, B. C. 301, with a detailed Account of the Campaigns of the Great Macedonian.   Boston, Houghton, Mifflin
& Co., 1890.   O. $5.00.

Freeman, E. A., The Chief Periods of European History.   Six lectures read in the
University of Oxford in Trinity Term, 1885, with an Essay on Greek Cities
under Roman Rule.   New York, Macmillan & Co., 1886.   O. $2.50.

Mahaffy, J. P., The Greek World under Roman Sway.   From Polybius to Plutarch.
New York, Macmillan & Co., 1890.   D. $3.00.

Freeman, E. A., The History of Sicily, from the Earliest Times.   New York, Macmillan & Co., 1891–95.   4 volumes.   O. $21.50.   (Volume IV. is edited from
posthumus MSS. with supplement and notes by Arthur J. Evans.)

Freeman, E. A., Greater Greece and Greater Britain and George Washington, the
Expander of England.   New York, Macmillan & Co., 1886.   D. $1.00.

Freeman, E. A., History of Federal Government from the Foundation of the Achaian
League to the Disruption of the United States.   Volume I.   General Intro-
duction—History of Greek Federations.   New York, Macmillan & Co., 1863.
O. $3.75.

Felton, C. C., Greece, Ancient and Modern.   Lectures delivered before the Lowell
Institute.   New edition.   Boston, Houghton, Mifflin & Co., 1886.   O. $5.00.

Gardner, P., New Chapters in Greek History.   Historical Results of Recent Excavations in Greece and Asia Minor.   New York, G. P. Putnam's Sons, 1892.
O. $5.00.

Mahaffy, J. P., Problems in Greek History.   New York, Macmillan & Co., 1892.
D. $2.50.

C. ROME.

De Quincey, Thos., Philosophy of Roman History.   In Volume VI. of his Collected
Writings; edited by D. Masson, New York, Macmillan & Co., 1890. O. $1.25.

Tighe, A., The Development of the Roman Constitution.   New York, D. Appleton
& Co., 1886.   S. $ .35.

Duruy, V., History of Rome and the Roman People from its Origin to the Establishment of the Christian Empire [313 A. D.]; translated by Mr. Clarke and
Miss Ripley, and edited by J. P. Mahaffy.   Boston, Estes & Lauriat, 1883–86.
6 volumes. $6.00 each.

Merivale, C., A General History of Rome, from the Foundation of the City to the
Fall of Augustulus [753 B. C.–476 A. D.].   New York, D. Appleton & Co.,
1876.   D. $2.00.

Pelham, H. F., Outlines of Roman History.   New York, G. P. Putnam's Sons, 1893.
O. $1.75.

Gilman, A., The Story of Rome.   New York, G. P. Putnam's Sons, 1885. O. $1.50.

Allen, W. F., A Short History of the Roman People.   Boston, Ginn & Co., 1890.
D. $1.00.

Mommsen, Th., The History of Rome; translated with the Sanction of the Author
by W. P. Dickson.   New edition, revised throughout and embodying recent
additions.   New York, Charles Scribner's Sons, 1896.   5 volumes.   O. $10.00.

Liddell, H. G., A History of Rome, from the Earliest Times to the Establishment of the Empire. With chapters on the history of Literature and Art. New York, Harper Bros. & Co., 1863. D. $1.25.

Arnold, T., History of Rome. 5th edition. London, H. Bickers & Son, 1882. 24s.

Ihne, Wm., The History of Rome. English Edition. New York, Longmans, Green & Co., 1871–82. 5 volumes. O. 77s.

Ihne, Wm., Early Rome, from the Foundation of the City to its Destruction by the Gauls. (*In the* "Epochs of Ancient History" Series.) 4th edition. New York, Charles Scribner's Sons, 1886. D. $1.00.

Arnold, T., The Second Punic War; edited by W. T. Arnold. New York, Macmillan & Co., 1886. O. $2.25.

Smith, R. Bosworth, Rome and Carthage. The Punic Wars. 5th edition. (*In the* "Epochs of Ancient History" Series.) New York, Charles Scribner's Sons, 1881. D. $1.00.

Church, A. J., (*with the collaboration of* A. Gilman), The Story of Carthage. New York, G. P. Putnam's Sons, 1888. O. $1.50.

Dodge, T. A., Hannibal. A History of the Art of War among the Carthaginians and Romans down to the Battle of Pydna, 168 B. C., with a Detailed Account of the Second Punic War. Boston, Houghton, Mifflin & Co., 1891. O. $5.00.

Long, Geo., The Decline of the Roman Republic. New York, Macmillan & Co., 1864–74. 5 volumes. O. $7.50.

Beesly, A. H., The Gracchi, Marius and Sulla. (*In the* "Epochs of Ancient History" Series). New York, Charles Scribner's Sons, 1887. D. $1.00.

Merivale, C., The Roman Triumvirates. (*Same Series.*) 5th edition. 1887. D. $1.00.

Merivale, C., The Fall of the Roman Republic. 2d edition. 1853. D. $2.25.

Strachan-Davidson, J. L., Cicero and the Fall of the Roman Republic. New York, G. P. Putnam's Sons, 1894. D. $1.50.

Fowler, W. W., Julius Cæsar and the Foundation of the Roman Imperial System. New York, G. P. Putnam's Sons, 1892. D. $1.50.

Merivale, C., History of the Romans under the Empire. New York, Longmans, Green & Co., 1890. 8 volumes. $10.00. [*A new edition is in preparation.*]

Capes, W. W., Roman History—The Early Empire; from the Assassination of Julius Cæsar to that of Domitian. 6th edition. (*In the* "Epochs of Ancient History" Series.) New York, Charles Scribner's Sons, 1887. D. $1.00.

De Quincey, Thos., The Cæsars. In Volume VI. of his Collected Writings; edited by D. Masson. New York, Macmillan & Co., 1890. O. $1.25.

Capes, W. W., The Roman Empire of the Second Century, or the Age of the Antonines. (*In the* "Epochs of Ancient History" Series.) 4th edition. 1887. D. $1.00.

Gibbon, Edward, History of the Decline and Fall of the Roman Empire. New York, Harper Bros. & Co., 1880. 6 volumes. O. $12.00. [A new edition, edited by J. B. Bury, is in course of publication, to be completed in 7 volumes; Volumes I., II., $2.00 per volume. The Macmillan Company.]

Sheppard, J. G., The Fall of Rome and the Rise of the New Nationalities. A Series of Lectures on the Connection between Ancient and Modern History. London, 1861; New York, Geo. Routledge & Sons, 1892. D. $1.50.

Bryce, J., The Holy Roman Empire. 8th edition, revised. New York, Macmillan & Co., 1895. O. $1.00.

Emerton, E., An Introduction to the Study of the Middle Ages. Boston, Ginn &
Co., 1888. D. $1.25.

Emerton, E., Mediæval Europe (814-1300 A. D.). Boston, Ginn & Co., 1894.
D. $1.65.

Hodgkin, T., Italy and Her Invaders (376-744 A. D.). New York, Macmillan &
Co., 1880-95. 6 volumes. O. $32.00.

Bury, J. B., A History of the Later Roman Empire from Arcadius to Irene (395-
800 A. D.). New York, Macmillan & Co., 1889. 2 volumes. O. $6.00.

Bury, J. B., A History of the Roman Empire from its Foundation to the Death of
Marcus Aurelius (27 B. C.-180 A. D.). New York, Harper & Bros., 1893.
D. $1.50.

Seeley, J. R., Roman Imperialism. In his Lectures and Essays. New York, Macmillan & Co., 1870. O. $1.00.

Bradley, H., The Story of the Goths, from the Earliest Times to the End of the
Gothic Dominion in Spain. New York, G. P. Putnam's Sons, 1891. O.
$1.50.

Scarth, H. M., Early Britain—Roman Britain. London, Society for the Promotion
of Christian Knowledge, 1883. D. 2s. 6d.

Wright, T., The Celt, the Roman and the Saxon. A History of the Early Inhabit-
ants of Britain. 4th edition. London, Kegan Paul, Trench, Trübner & Co.,
1885. O. 9s.

Kingsley, C., The Roman and the Teuton. A Series of Lectures delivered before
the University of Cambridge. New edition, with a preface by Max Müller.
New York, Macmillan & Co., 1887. O. $1.25.

Arnold, W. T., The Roman System of Provincial Administration. New York,
Macmillan & Co., 1879. O. (Out of print.)

Mommsen, Th., The Provinces of the Roman Empire from Cæsar to Diocletian;
translated with the author's sanction and additions by W. P. Dickson. New
York, Charles Scribners' Sons, 1886. 2 volumes. O. $6.00.

Milman, H. H., Complete Works. Including: (a) The History of the Jews (2
volumes), (b) The History of Christianity to the Abolition of Paganism (2
volumes), (c) History of Latin Christianity (4 volumes). New York, Charles
Scribner's Sons, 1883. O. $12.00.

Gregorovius, Ferd., History of the City of Rome in the Middle Ages; translated
from the 4th German edition by Annie Hamilton. New York, Macmillan &
Co., 1894—. Volumes I. and II., (to 800 A. D.), $3.75., Vol. III., $2.00.,
Vol. IV., 2 pts., $3.00. D.

c. Political Antiquities.

Fowler, W. W., The City-State of the Greeks and Romans. A Survey Introductory
to the Study of Ancient History. New York, Macmillan & Co., 1893. S. $1.00.

Morey, W. C., Outlines of Roman Law, comprising its Historical Growth and General Principles. 8th edition. New York, G. P. Putnam's Sons, 1896. O.
$1.75.

Forsyth, Wm., Hortensius; or, The Advocate. An Historical Essay. 3d edition.
London, J. Murray, 1879. O. 7s. 6d.

Gilbert, G., The Constitutional Antiquities of Sparta and Athens; translated by E. J.
Brooks and T. Nicklin, with an introductory note by J. E. Sandys. New
York, Macmillan & Co., 1895. O. $3.00.

Boeckh, A., The Public Economy of the Athenians, with notes and a copious index; translated from the 2d German edition by A. Lamb. Boston, Little, Brown & Co., 1857. O. (*Out of print.*)

Schömann, G. F., The Antiquities of Greece. The State; translated from the German by E. G. Hardy and J. S. Mann. London, Rivingtons, 1880. 10s.

Greenidge, A. H. J., A Handbook of Greek Constitutional History. New York, The Macmillan Co., 1896. O. $1.25.

Judson, H. P., Cæsar's Army: A Study of the Military Art of the Romans in the Last Days of the Republic. Boston, Ginn & Co., 1888. D. $1.10.

VI. PRIVATE AFFAIRS.

Compayré, G., The History of Pedagogy; translated, with an introduction, notes and an index, by W. H. Payne. Boston, D. C. Heath & Co., 1896. O. $1.75.

Davidson, T., The Education of the Greek People and its Influence on Civilisation. New York, D. Appleton & Co., 1894. D. $1.50. [International Education Series.]

Mahaffy, J. P., Old Greek Education. New York, Harper & Bros., 1882. S. .75.

Capes, W. W., University Life in Ancient Athens; being the Substance of Four Oxford Lectures. New York, Harper & Bros., 1877. Th. $0.25.

Evans, Maria M., Chapters on Greek Dress. New York, Macmillan & Co., 1893. O. $2.00.

Mahaffy, J. P., Social Life in Greece from Homer to Menander. 7th edition. New York, Macmillan & Co., 1890. D. $2.50.

Mahaffy, J. P., Greek Life and Thought from the Age of Alexander to the Roman Conquest. (*Sequel to the preceding.*) New York, Macmillan & Co., 1887. D. $3.50.

Inge, W. R., Society in Rome under the Cesars. New York, Charles Scribner's Sons, 1888. O. $1.25.

Church, A. J., Roman Life in the Days of Cicero. Sketches drawn from his Letters and Speeches. New York, Dodd, Mead & Co., 1884. O. $1.00.

Blümner, H., The Home Life of the Ancient Greeks; translated from the German by Alice Zimmern. New York, Cassell Publishing Co., 1893. O. $2.00.

Church, A. J., Pictures from Roman Life and Story. New York, D. Appleton & Co., 1892. O. $1.50.

Preston, Harriet W., and Dodge, Louise, The Private Life of the Romans. Boston, Leach, Shewell & Sanborn, 1894. D. $1.00.

VII. THE FINE ARTS.

a. Histories of the Arts.

Lübke, W., Outlines of the History of Art; a new translation from the 7th German edition. Edited by C. Cook. American edition. New York, Dodd, Mead & Co., 1878. 2 volumes. Large O. $14.00.

Winckelmann, J. J., The History of Ancient Art; translated from the German by G. H. Lodge. Boston, Houghton, Mifflin & Co., 1880. 4 volumes in 2. O. $9.00.

von Reber, F., History of Ancient Art; translated and augmented by J. T. Clarke. New York, Harper & Bros., 1883. O. $3.50.

Lübke, W., History of Sculpture from the Earliest Ages to the Present Time ; translated by F. E. Bunnètt. Philadelphia, J. B. Lippincott and Co., 1872. 2 volumes. Large O. $18.00.

Mitchell, Lucy, M., A History of Ancient Sculpture. New York, Dodd, Mead & Co., 1883. Q. $12.50. *Cheap edition*. 1888. $7.50.

Murray, A. S., A History of Greek Sculpture. Revised edition. London, John Murray, 1890. 2 volumes. O. $14.00.

Gardner, E. A., A Handbook of Greek Sculpture. New York, The Macmillan Co., Part I., 1896 ; Part II., 1897. D. $2.50.

Harrison, Jane E., Introductory Studies in Greek Art. New York, Macmillan & Co., 1885. O. $2.25.

Perrot, G. and Chipiez, C., History of Art in Primitive Greece. Mycenian Art ; translated from the French. London, Chapman & Hall, 1894. 2 volumes. Q. $15.50.

Tsountas, Chr., and Manatt, J. I., The Mycenaean Age. A Study of the Monu·ments and Culture of Pre-Homeric Greece. With an introduction by Dr. Dörpfeld. Boston, Houghton, Mifflin & Co., 1897. O. $6.00.

Furtwängler, A., Masterpieces of Greek Sculpture. A Series of Essays on the History of Art ; edited by Eugénie Sellers with 19 full-page plates and 200 text engravings. New York, Charles Scribner's Sons, 1895. Q. $15.00.

Waldstein, C., Essays on the Art of Pheidias. New York, Century Co., 1885. O. $7.50.

Gardner, P., The Types of Greek Coins. An Archæological Essay. New York, Macmillan & Co., 1883. F. $8.00.

Woltmann, A. and Woermann, K., History of Painting ; edited from the German by Sidney Colvin. New York, Dodd, Mead & Co., 1880–1887. 2 volumes. Q. *Cheap edition*. $7.50.

Fergusson, J., A History of Architecture in all Countries from the Earliest Times to the Present Day. 2d edition. Volume I. Boston, Little, Brown & Co., 1874. O. $12.00.

Durm, J., Die Baukunst der Griechen. 2d edition. Darmstadt, Bergstræsser, 1892. 20 M.

Jackquemart, A., History of the Ceramic Art. A Descriptive and Philosophical Study of the Pottery of all Ages and all Nations ; translated by Mrs. Bury Palliser. 2d edition. New York, Charles Scribner's Sons, 1877. O. $10.50.

Monro, D. B., The Modes of Ancient Greek Music. New York, Macmillan & Co., 1894. O. $2.50.

b. Descriptive Handbooks, etc., of Archæology and Art.

Baumeister, A. (*editor*), Denkmäler des klassischen Altertums. Zur Erläuterung des Lebens der Griechen und Römer in Religion, Kunst und Sitte. Munich, Oldenbourg, 1885–88. 3 volumes. Q. (*Can be bought for about* 45 M.)

Baedeker, K., Handbooks for travellers. Leipzig, Karl Baedeker :

> Part I. Northern Italy. Including Leghorn, Florence, Ravenna and routes through Switzerland and Austria. 10th remodeled edition. 1894. S. 8 M. b.
>
> Part II. Central Italy and Rome. 11th revised edition. 1893. S. 6 M. b.
>
> Part III. Southern Italy and Sicily. With excursions to the Lipari Islands,

Malta, Sardinia, Tunis and Corfu. 12th revised edition. 1896. S. 6 M. b.

Middleton, J. H., The Remains of Ancient Rome. New York, Macmillan & Co., 1892. 2 volumes. O. $7.00.

Burn, R., Ancient Rome and Its Neighborhood. An Illustrated Handbook of the Ruins of the City. New York, Macmillan & Co., 1895. $2.25.

Ziegler, C., Das alte Rom. (*18 colored plates and 5 woodcuts, with text.*) Stuttgart, Neff, 1882. Q. 4.50 M. b.

Schneider, A., Das alte Rom. Entwickelung seines Grundrisses und Geschichte seiner Bauten auf 12 Karten und 14 Tafeln dargestellt und mit einem Plane der heutigen Stadt so wie einer stadtgeschichtlichen Einleitung. Leipzig, B. G. Teubner, 1896. F. 16 M. b.

Lanciani, R., Ancient Rome in the Light of Recent Discoveries. New York, Houghton, Mifflin & Co., 1889. O. $6.00.

Murray, J., A Handbook of Rome and its Environs. 14th edition. London, J. Murray, 1887. 19s.

Hare, A. J. C., Walks in Rome. 16th edition. New York, Geo. Routledge & Sons. O. $3.50.

Hare, A. J. C., Days near Rome; 3d edition. New York, Geo. Routledge & Sons, 1884. 2 volumes. O. $5.00.

Taine, H., Italy, Naples and Rome; translated from the French by J. Durand. New York, Henry Holt & Co., 1875. O. $2.50.

Lanciani, R., Pagan and Christian Rome. New York, Houghton, Mifflin & Co., 1893. O. $6.00.

Dyer, T. H., Pompeii, 4th edition. New York, Macmillan & Co., 1891. D. $2.25.

Dennis, G., The Cities and Cemeteries of Etruria. Revised edition recording the most recent discoveries. London, J. Murray, 1883. 2 volumes. O. 21s.

Baedeker, K., Greece. Handbook for Travelers. 2d revised edition. Leipzig, K. Baedeker, 1894. S. 8 M. b.

Harrison, Jane E., Mythology and Monuments of Ancient Athens. Being a translation of a portion of the "Attica" of Pausanias by Margaret de G. Verrall. With introductory essay and archæological commentary by Jane E. Harrison. New York, Macmillan & Co., 1890. D. $4.00.

Schuchhardt, C., Schliemann's Excavations. An Archæological and Historical Study; translated from the German by Eugénie Sellers. With an appendix on the recent discoveries at Hissarlik by Dr. Schliemann and Dr. Dörpfeld and an introduction by Walter Leaf. New York, Macmillan & Co., 1891. O. $4.00.

Diehl, C., Excursions in Greece to recently Explored Sites of Classical Interest. A popular account of the results of recent excavations; translated by Emma R. Perkins. With an introduction by R. S. Poole. New York, B. Westermann (*importer*), 1893. O. $2.00.

Mahaffy, J. P., Rambles and Studies in Greece. 3d edition. New York, Macmillan & Co., 1887. D. $3.00.

Dyer, T. H., Ancient Athens. Its History, Topography and Remains. London, Bell & Daldy, 1873. O. 25s.

Newton, C. T., Essays on Art and Archæology. New York, Macmillan & Co., 1880. O. $4.00.

Murray, A. S., Handbook of Greek Archæology. Vases, Bronzes, Gems, Sculpture, Terra-Cottas, Mural Paintings, Architecture, etc., with numerous illustrations. New York, Charles Scribner's Sons, 1892. O. $5.00.

Burn, R., Roman Literature in Relation to Roman Art. New York, Macmillan & Co., 1888. O. $2.25.

VIII. PHILOSOPHY AND SCIENCE.

Zeller, Ed., The Philosophy of the Greeks. New edition. New York, Longmans, Green & Co., 1868-97. 7 volumes.

> Vols. I-II. A History of Greek Philosophy from the Earliest Period to the Time of Socrates, with a general introduction ; translated from the German by Sarah F. Alleyne. $10.00.
>
> Vol. III. Socrates and the Socratic Schools ; translated from the German by O. J. Reichel. $3.50.
>
> Vol. IV. Plato and the Older Academy ; translated from the German by Sarah F. Alleyne and A. Goodwin. $6.00.
>
> Vol. V. Aristotle and the Earlier Peripatetics ; translated from the German by B. F. C. Costelloe and T. H. Muirhead. (*In two volumes.*)
>
> Vol. VI. The Stoics, Epicureans and Sceptics ; translated from the German by O. J. Reichel. $5.00.
>
> Vol. VII. A History of Eclecticism in Greek Philosophy ; translated from the German by Sarah F. Alleyne. $3.50.

Zeller, Ed., Outlines of the History of Greek Philosophy ; translated by Sarah F. Alleyne and E. Abbott. New York, Henry Holt & Co., 1886. O. $1.75. (*Epitome of the above.*)

Ueberweg, Fr., History of Philosophy from Thales to the Present Time ; translated from the 4th German edition by Geo. S. Morris. With additions by Noah Porter. Volume I. History of the Ancient and Mediæval Philosophy. New York, Charles Scribner's Sons, 1889. O. $2.50.

Burt, B. C., A Brief History of Greek Philosophy. Boston, Ginn & Co., 1889. D. $1.25.

Ferrier, T. F., Philosophical Works. Volume II. Lectures on Greek Philosophy. 4th edition. London, Wm. Blackwood & Sons, 1882. O. 10s. 6d.

Pater, W., Plato and Platonism. A Series of Lectures. New York, Macmillan & Co., 1893. D. $1.75.

Osborn, H. F., From the Greeks to Darwin. An Outline of the Development of the Evolution Idea. (Columbia University Biological Series.) New York, Macmillan & Co., 1894. O. $2.00.

IX. MISCELLANEOUS ESSAYS.

Butcher, S. H., Some Aspects of the Greek Genius. 2d edition. New York, Macmillan & Co., 1894. D. $2.50.

Story, W. W., Excursions in Art and Letters. Boston, Houghton, Mifflin & Co., 1891. D. $1.25.

Symonds, J. A., Sketches and Studies in Southern Europe. New York, Harper & Bros., 1880. 2 volumes. D. $4.00.

Rydberg, V., Roman Days ; from the Swedish by A. C. Clark. With a sketch of Rydberg by A. H. W. Lindehn. 2d edition. New York, G. P. Putnam's Sons, 1887. D. $2.00.

Myers, F. W. H., Classical Essays. New York, Macmillan & Co., 1888. $1.25.

Abbott, E. A., Hellenica. A Collection of Essays on Greek Poetry, Philosophy, History and Religion. London, Rivingtons, 1880. O. 16s.

Pater, W., Greek Studies. A Series of Essays; prepared for the press by C. S. Shadwell. New York, Macmillan & Co., 1895. O. $1.25.

Kingsley, C., Historical Lectures and Essays. In volume XVI. of his Works. New York, Macmillan & Co., 1880. O. $1.25.

Freeman, E. A., Historical Essays. 2d series. (3d edition.) 3d series. New York, Macmillan & Co., 1873–79. 2 volumes. O. $3.00.

Freeman, E. A., Historical and Architectural Sketches : chiefly Italian. New York, Macmillan & Co., 1876. O. $3.00.

X. INFLUENCE OF GREECE AND ROME.

Hatch, E., The Influence of Greek Ideas and Usages upon the Christian Church; edited by A. M. Fairbairn [*Hibbert Lectures*]. 3d edition. London, Williams & Norgate, 1891. O. 10s. 6d.

Renan, E., On the Influence of the Institutions, Thought and Culture of Rome on Christianity, and the Development of the Catholic Church; translated by Charles Beard. London, Williams & Norgate, 1884. O. 10s. 6d.

Story, W. W., Roba di Roma. 8th edition. Boston, Houghton, Mifflin & Co., 1887. D. $2.50.

Gladstone, W. E., Place of Ancient Greece, in the Providential Order. In his "Gleanings of Past Years," Volume VII. New York, Charles Scribner's Sons, 1879. S. $1.00.

Davidson, T. *See under " Private Affairs," Section VI.*

Symonds, J. A., The Renaissance in Italy : The Revival of Learning. New York, Henry Holt & Co., 1888. O. $3.50.

Voigt, G., Die Wiederbelebung des Classischen Alterthums, oder das erste Jahrhundert des Humanismus. 3 Auflage besorgt von M. Lehnerdt. Berlin, Reimer, 1893. 20.00 M. b.

XI. ENGLISH NOVELS, ETC., ILLUSTRATING THE LIFE OF CLASSICAL ANTIQUITY.

Browning, Cleon, Balaustion's Adventure; **Byron**, Childe Harold's Pilgrimage ; **Chaucer**, Legende of Goode Women; **Church**, 2,000 Years Ago; **Ebers**, Homo Sum, Serapis, The Emperor, The Egyptian Princess; **Eckstein**, Nero, Prusius, Quintus Claudius, The Chaldean Magician; **Herbert**, The Roman Traitor ; **Kingsley**, Hypatia; **Knowles**, Virginius; **Landor**, Pericles and Aspasia, Imaginary Conversations, Poems ; **Lang**, Helen of Troy, Letters to Dead Authors ; **Lockhart**, Valerius ; **Lytton**, Last Days of Pompeii ; **Macauley**, Lays of Ancient Rome, ed. W. J. and J. C. Rolfe ; **Morris, L.**, The Epic of Hades ; **Morris, W.**, Earthly Paradise, Life and Death of Jason ; **Newman**, Callista ; **Pater**, Marius the Epicurean; **Richardson**, The Son of a Star ; **Rydberg**, The Last Athenian ; **Sienkiewicz**, Quo Vadis, A Narrative of the Time of Nero ; **Shakespeare**, Troilus and Cressida and other dramas; **Swinburne**, Atalanta in Calydon ; **Taylor**, Antinous ; **Wallace**, Ben-Hur **Ware**, Aurelian, Julian, Zenobia ; **Westbury**, Acte ; **Wiseman**, Fabiola.

VALUABLE WORKS OF REFERENCE

An Atlas of Classical Antiquities
By T. SCHREIBER
Edited for English use by Professor W. C. F. ANDERSON
Oblong 4to. **$6.50**

A Dictionary of Classical Antiquities
Mythology, Religion, Literature and Art
Edited from the German of **DR. SEYFFERT**, with Additions, by the late
HENRY NETTLESHIP, M.A., and J. E. SANDYS, Litt.D.
With 450 fine Illustrations. 8vo. **$3.00**

Greek History
From its Origin to the Destruction of the Independence of the Greek People
By ADOLF HOLM
Authorized Translation. Volumes I., II. and III., **$2.50** each
Volume IV., *in the Press*

A History of Classical Greek Literature
By J. P. MAHAFFY

Vol. I. **Greek Poetry.** (In two parts.) Part I. The Poets. With an Appendix on Homer by Prof. SAYCE. Third Edition, Revised and Enlarged. 12mo. Part II. The Dramatic Poets. Third Edition, Revised and Enlarged. **$2.25**

Vol. II. **Greek Prose.** (In two parts.) Part I. From Herodotus to Plato. Part II. From Isocrates to Aristotle. 12mo. Cloth, gilt, **$2.25**
The four volumes in case, **$4.50**

A History of Classical Roman Literature
By WILLIAM Y. SELLAR, M. A.

The Roman Poets of the Republic. Third Edition, Enlarged. **$2.50**
The Roman Poets of the Augustan Age. Virgil. Second Edition. **$2.25**

The Roman Poets of the Augustan Age. Horace and the Elegiac Poets. With a Memoir of the author by ANDREW LANG, M.A., and a Portrait. 8vo. **$3.50**

PUBLISHED BY

THE MACMILLAN COMPANY
66 Fifth Avenue, New York

To be Published Shortly in Six Volumes, 8vo.
Illustrated with many Maps, Plans, and Engravings. Price, $25.00 Net.

Pausanias's Description of Greece

TRANSLATED WITH A COMMENTARY BY J. G. FRAZER, M.A., LL.D.,
(GLASGOW), FELLOW OF TRINITY COLLEGE, CAMBRIDGE.

THE WORK IS DIVIDED AS FOLLOWS:

Vol. I.—Introduction. Translation. Critical Notes on the Greek text.
II.—Commentary on Book I (Attica).
III.—Commentary on Books II–V (Argolis, Laconia, Messenia, Elis I).
IV.—Commentary on Books VI–VIII (Elis II, Achaia, Arcadia).
V.—Commentary on Books IX, X (Boeotia, Phocis). Addenda.
VI.—Indices. Maps.

** *The Volumes will not be sold separately.*

IN this work, the fruit of not a few days of labour, my aim has been to give, first, a faithful and idiomatic rendering of Pausanias, and, second, a Commentary which shall illustrate his description of ancient Greece by the light of modern research. It is safe to say that for no Greek author have the illustrative materials been accumulated in such profusion as for Pausanias. Within the present century Greece has been explored by a succession of scholarly travellers, many of its most important sites have been excavated, its buildings measured and described, its artistic treasures collected, compared, and criticized. The many-sided results of these researches are dispersed and too often buried in a motley multitude of publications — in learned journals and the proceedings and transactions of Societies, Academies, and Institutions, as well as in an almost endless array of separate books and pamphlets. To collect from these multifarious sources the scattered rays of light and to concentrate them on Pausanias or rather on his subject, ancient Greece, has been one of my chief objects in writing the Commentary. My general purpose has been to present a fairly complete picture of ancient Greece, its monuments and its scenery, so far as that can be done from a study of the descriptions of classical authors, the existing remains of antiquity, and the appearance of the country at the present day. The better to fit myself for the task I had set myself, I have paid two visits, each of nearly three months, have travelled in all the provinces except Locris and seen most of the chief sites described by Pausanias. I have thus been able to describe much of the scenery and many of the ruins at first hand and to supplement on certain points the accounts of former travellers, especially in some of the more rarely visited parts of Arcadia, Boeotia, and Phocis. Lastly I have attempted occasionally to illustrate Pausanias's references to Greek myths and religion by adducing parallels from the religion and folk-lore of other peoples ; but I have kept this side of the subject in strict subordination to the topographical and archæological, and I have seldom been tempted to launch out on the wide and troubled sea of mythological speculation. * * *

But while I have aimed at producing a book which shall meet the requirements of scholars, I have tried at the same time, without any sacrifice of accuracy, to make it intelligible to all educated readers, whether they are classical scholars or not. For it seemed to me that every educated person must have some interest in picturing to himself how ancient Greece, the mother of so much of our modern civilization, may have looked, if not in the meridian splendour, at least in the peaceful evenings of her days, while she was still rich in the artistic treasures of the past and had not yet been stripped of her glories and left ruined and bare by the ravages of barbarians and the still more destructive fanaticism of a new religion. Hence I have been at pains to write as simply and clearly as I could, to avoid all unnecessary technicalities, and to give all quotations from Greek and other foreign languages in English.

J. G. FRAZER.

THE MACMILLAN COMPANY, 66 Fifth Ave., New York

RECOMMENDED FOR A

HIGH SCHOOL CLASSICAL LIBRARY

BY A COMMITTEE OF THE

Michigan Schoolmasters' Club.

This list is presented with the compliments of Sheehan & Co., University Booksellers, Ann Arbor, Michigan, by whom the books here mentioned are kept in stock, and will be mailed to any address at lowest wholesale prices.

ANN ARBOR:
SHEEHAN & COMPANY,
1895.

NOTE.

This committee, by whom the following list was selected, was appointed at the Spring Meeting of the Michigan Schoolmasters' Club in March, 1894. It consists of the following members: Mr. Clarence L. Meader, Instructor in Latin in the University of Michigan, No. 9 East University Avenue, Ann Arbor, Michigan, chairman; Prof. B. L. D'Ooge, of the Michigan State Normal School, Ypsilanti, Mich.; Principal E. C. Warriner, of the Battle Creek High School; Principal E. B. Sherman, of the Bay City High School.

Grateful acknowledgment of the committee for much kind help in their work is due to Professors F. W. Kelsey, M. L. D'Ooge, J. C. Rolfe, and Assistant Professor J. H. Drake, of the University of Michigan; Mr. Lawrence C. Hull, of Lawrenceville, N. J.; Mr. H. D. Sanders, Mr. H. F. DeCou, and Mr. George Rebec, of the University of Michigan; Professor Walter Miller, of Leland Stanford, Jr., University; Mr. Isaac B. Burgess, of Morgan Park, Ill.; Professor Alfred Gudeman, University of Pennsylvania; Professor Sidney G. Ashmore, Union College; Professor C. M. Moss, University of Illinois; Professor Walter Bridgman, Lake Forest, Ill.; Professor Charles Forster Smith, University of Wisconsin; Mr. W. W. Bishop, Northwestern University Academy, Evanston, Ill.; Professors S. J. Axtell and Samuel Brooks, of Kalamazoo College; Principal J. O. Hartwell, of the Kalamazoo High School; Mr. Charles B. Gleason, of Redlands, California; Mr. W. D. Baker, Battle Creek High School; Mr. F. W. Townsend, Superintendent of Schools, Marshall, Mich., and Principal Ralph Garwood, Marshall, Mich.

The thanks of the committee are also due to Mr. John V. Sheehan for his kind interest in providing for the publication of the list.

The following abbreviations are to be noted: f., *folio;* b., *bound* (all *German* publications not so marked are sold unbound); tr., *translated* or *translated by;* Gk., *Greek;* Lat., *Latin;* M., *Mark* or *Marks*, 25c; R., *Roman;* B., *Boston:* Leip., *Leipzig;* L., *London.*

The abbreviations *Crit. ap., Eng. notes or Ger. notes,* following the name of an editor in sections III., *a*, B. and III., *b*, B. indicate that the editions cited are provided with a critical apparatus, English notes or German notes respectively. Editions not so marked are either simple text editions or have brief critical notes.

Publishers: Allyn & B(*acon, Boston*); D. App(*leton & Co., New York*); (*Geo.*) Bell (*& Sons, London*); Dodd, (*Mead & Co., New York*); Ginn (*& Co., Boston*); Harper (*& Bros., New York*); (*D. C.*) Heath (*& Co., Boston*); (*Henry*) Holt (*& Co., New York*); H(*oughton*), M(*ifflin*) & Co., (*Boston and New York*); Keagan Paul, (*Trench, Truebner & Co., London*); L(*each*) S(*hewell*) & S(*anborn, Boston*); Lee & S(*hepard, Boston*); Lipp(*incott & Co., Philadelphia*); Little, B(*rown*), & Co., (*Boston*); Long(*mans, Green & Co., London and New York*); Macmillan *& Co., London and New York*); (*J.*) Parker (*& Co., London*); Putnam's *Sons, New York and London*); Rivington, (*Percivale & Co., London*); (*Geo.*) Routledge (*& Sons, New York*); Scribner('*s Sons, New York*).

CARD.

Messrs. Sheehan & Co., Ann Arbor, Michigan, beg to inform teachers and school boards that they keep in stock, not only the books of the inclosed list,' but also a full line of college and high school text books. French and German books are imported direct. They have also a full line of athletic and gymnasium goods, suitable for college and high school students.

Those who receive this list are requested to read the " Report of the Committee on the High School Classical Library " given at the Classical Conference in March, 1895, and published in The School Review for June. (Copies may be obtained by remitting 20 cents to Principal C. H. Thurber, Colgate Academy, Hamilton, New York.) The principles of selection are there stated.

N. B.—The double asterisk (**) is prefixed to the titles of books which should be found on the shelves of EVERY *high school classical library. Books which are somewhat less essential are indicated by the single asterisk. The purchase of the entire list is strongly recommended.*

I. BOOKS OF REFERENCE, HANDBOOKS, ETC.

**Kiepert, H., Atlas Antiquus. 4°. Leach, Shewell & Sanborn. $2.00.

Huelsen, Ch., The Roman Forum. 2 plates. 4°. Rome. Spithoeer. 1892. 2.50 M.

**Engelmann-Anderson, Pictorial Atlas to Homer's Il. and Od. f. N. Y. B. Westermann & Co. $3.00.

Kampen, A. von, XV ad Cæsaris de Bello Gallico Commentarios Tabulæ. Gotha. 1879. 1.80 M.

Oehler, R., Bilder-Atlas zu Cæsar. 8°. Leipzig. 1890. 4 M. b.

**Schreiber, Th., Atlas of Classical Antiquities. 4°. N. Y. Macmillan & Co. 1894. $6.50.

Seemann, A., Kultur-Atlas. 8°. Leipzig. 1886-94. 18 M.

Putzger, F. W., Historischer Schul-Atlas. f. Leipzig. 1894. 2.70 M. b.

**Liddell and Scott, Greek Lexicon. 7th ed. rev. N. Y. Harper & Bros. 1883. $10.00.

**Yonge, C. D., English-Greek Lexicon. 8°. Harper. 1886. $4.50.

Autenrieth, G., Homeric Dictionary. rev. ed. Harper. 1891. $1.10.

Thayer, J. H., Greek-Eng. Lexicon of the New Testament. 2d ed. 8°. Harper. 1888. $5.00.

**Harpers' Latin Lexicon. 4°. Harper. 1879. $6.00.

*Lewis, C. T., Latin Dictionary for Schools. 8°. Harper. 1889. $5.50.

**Lewis, C. T., Elementary Latin Dictionary. 8°. Harper. 1891. $2.00.

**White, J. T., Lat.-Eng. and Eng.-Lat. Dictionary. 8th ed. B. Ginn & Co. 1884-2. $2.55.

Meissner, C., Latin Phrase-Book. tr. 12°. Macm. 1894. $1.10.

Merguet, H., Lexikon zu den Reden Ciceros. 4 vols. 8°. Jena. 1883-4. 60 M.

Merguet, H., Lexikon zu den Schriften Ciceros. vols. I.-III., 10. Jena. 1887—. 110+ M. (*now publishing.*)

Meusel, H., Lexicon Caesarianum. 2 vols. 4°. Berlin. 1887-93. 45 M.

*Boeckh, Aug., Encyclopädie und Methodologie der philologischen Wissenschaften. 2d ed. 8°. Leipzig. 1886. 14 M.

Reinach, S., Manuel de Philologie classique. 2 vols. Paris. Libraire Hachette. vol. I. 2d ed. 1883; vol. II. 1884. 15 Fr.

**Gudeman, A., Outlines of the History of Classical Philology. 2d ed. 8°. B. Ginn. 1895. $1.05.

**Huebner, E., Bibliographie der klassischen Altertumswissenschaft. 2d ed. 8°. Berlin. 1889. 15 M.

**Engelmann, Wm., Bibliotheca Scriptorum Classicorum. 2 vols. 8°. Leipzig. 1880-2. 36 M.

Kelsey, F. W., Fifty Topics in Roman Antiquities. 12°. B. Allyn & Bacon. 1891. $ .50. (bibliographical.)

*Mayor, J. B., Guide to the Choice of Classical Books. 3d ed. 8°. London. Macm. 1885. $1.25.

*Adams, C. K., Manual of Historical Literature. 3d ed. rev. 8°. Harper. 1889. $2.50.

**Classical Review (monthly periodical). B. Ginn 1887—. $3.00 per year.

American Journal of Philology (quarterly periodical). Baltimore. Friedenwald & Co. 1881—. $3.00 per year.

American Journal of Archæology (quarterly periodical). Princeton Press. 1885—. $5.00 per year.

Alaudæ (Latin journal). Aquila. Imported by L. Bohn, 351 East 52d St., N. Y. $ .60 per year.

**Smith, Wm., Dictionary of Gk. and R. Antiquities. 3d ed. rev. 2 vols. B. Little, Brown & Co. 1890-1. $14.00.

*Seyffert, O., Dictionary of Classical Antiquities. 8°. Macm. 1895. $3.00.

*Ramsay, W., Manual of R. Antiquities. 15th ed. N. Y. Scribner's Sons. 1895. $3.00.

*Rich, A., A Dictionary of R. and Gk. Antiquities. 3d ed. 8°. N. Y. Longmans, Green & Co. 1873. $2.50.

**Gow, J., A Companion to School Classics. 3d ed. Macm. 1893. $1.75.

**Smith, Wm., Dictionary of Gk. and R. Geography. 2 vols. B. Little, B. & Co., 1854-7. $12.00.

**Smith, Wm., Dict. of Gk. and R. Biography and Mythology. 3 vols. 8°. B. Little, B. & Co. 1844-9. $18.00.

*Guhl, E., and Koner, W., The Life of the Greeks and Romans. 8°. N. Y. D. Appleton & Co. 1889. $2.50.

Becker, W. A., Gallus tr. by F. Metcalf. 3d ed. 8°. Long. 1882. $2.50.

Becker, W. A., Charicles tr. by F. Metcalf. 3d ed. 8°. Long. 1882. $2.50.

Falke, J. von, Greece and Rome. f. N. Y. Henry Holt & Co. old ed. 1885. $15.00. new ed. 1886. $10.00.

*Mueller, Iwan von, Handbuch der klassischen Altertumswissenschaft:

Vol. I. 2 ed. Munich. 1892. 17 M. b. Grundlegung und Geschichte der Philologie by L. and H. L. Urlichs. Hermeneutik und Kritik. Fr. Blass. Palæographie. Fr. Blass. Griechische

Epigraphik. W. Larfeldt. Römische Epigraphik. E. Hübner.
Zeitrechnung. L. W. Unger. Griech. und römische Metrologie.
II. Nissen.

Vol. II. 2 ed. 1890. 15.50 M. b. Sprachwissenschaft. K. Brugmann,
Fr. Stolz, J. H. Schmalz, etc. Metrik. Gleditsch.

Vol. III. 1890. 18.50 M. b. Geschichte der Völker Vorder-Asiens.
Fr. Hommel. Geographie und Geschichte des griech. Alter-
tums. H. G. Lolling und R. Pöhlmann. Geographie und
Geschichte des römischen Altertums. J. Jung, B. Niese und
O. Richter (Topographie von Rom.)

Vol. IV. 1. 2 ed. 1892–3. 11.50 M. b. Die griech. Staats- und Rechtsaltertümer. G. Busolt, A. Bauer, A. Müller.

Vol. IV. 2. 2 ed. 1893. 9.80 M. b. Die römischen Staats- und Kriegsaltertümer. H. Schiller. Privataltertümer. M. Voigt.

Vol. V. I. 2 ed. 1894. 7.20 M. b. Mathematik, Naturwissenschaft
und wissenschaftliche Erdkunde. S. Günther. Geschichte
der Philosophie. W. Windelband.

Vol. V. 3. 1890. 8.20 M. b. Griech. Kultusaltertümer. P. Stengel.
Das Bühnenwesen. G. Oehmichen.

Vol. VI. 1. 1893. 5.50 M. b. Klassische Kunstarchäologie. Sittl.

Vol. VII. 2 ed. 1890. 15.20 M. b. Geschichte der griech. Litteratur. W. Christ.

Vol. VIII. 1, 2. 1890. 7.20 M. b. Geschichte der römischen Litteratur. M. Schanz.

Vol. IX. 1. 1891. 10.50 M. b. Geschichte der byzantinischen Litteratur. K. Krumbacher.

(*other volumes to follow.*)

II. GREEK AND LATIN LANGUAGES.

(*For bibliography see Henry's Comparative Grammar.*)

Paul, H., The Principles of the History of Language. tr. H. A. Strong.
8°. Macm. 1889. $3.00.

Whitney, W. D., Language and the Study of Language. 4th ed. 8°.
Scribner. 1884. $2.50.

**Whitney, W. D., Life and Growth of Language. 6th ed. App. 1892. $1.50.

Whitney, W. D., Oriental and Linguistic Studies. vol. I. 8°. N. Y.
Scribner. 1875. $2.50.

Taylor, I., Words and Places. 3d ed. 12°. Macm. 1873. $1.60.

*Delbrueck, B., A Critical Survey of the History and Methods of Compar-
ative Philology of the I.-E. Languages. tr. E. Channing. 8°. B.
Ginn. 1885. $1.00.

*Schrader, O., Prehistoric Antiquities of the Aryan Peoples. tr. 8° L.
Charles Griffin & Co. 1890. 21s.

*Brugmann, K., Comparative Grammar of the Indo-European Languages.
tr. 4 vols. N. Y. Westermann. $17.50.

Henry, Victor, Comparative Grammar of Greek and Latin. tr. Elliot and Nettleship. 12°. Macm. 1894. $1.90. (*5th Freneh ed. rev. 1895.*)

Schmidt, J. H. H., Rythmic and Metric. tr. J. W. White. 8°. B. Ginn. $2.50.

Weil, H., L'Ordre des Mots....tr. Super. 8°. B. Ginn. 1887. $1.25.

Taylor, I., The Alphabet. 2 vols. 8°. Keagan Paul. 1883. 36s.

Kuehner, R., Ausführliche Grammatik der griechischen Sprache. 8°. Hanover. vol. I. 3d ed. vol. II. 2d ed. Leipzig. 1886-92. 27 M.

Meyer, G., Griechische Grammatik. 8°. 2d ed. Leipzig. 1886. 11 M.

Goodwin, W. W., Greek Moods and Tenses. 8°. B. Ginn. 1890. $2.15.

Seymour, T. D., Homeric Language and Verse. 12°. B. Ginn. 1885. $.80.

Monro, D. B., A Grammar of the Homeric Dialect. 2d ed. 8°. Macm. 1891. $3.50.

Blass, Fr., Pronunciation of Ancient Greek. tr. W. J. Purton. 8°. Macm. 1890. $1.90.

Veitch, W., Greek Verbs Irregular and Defective. 8°. 4th ed. Macm. 1887. $2.50.

Roberts, E. S., Introduction to Gk. Epigraphy. Part I. 8°. Macm. 1887. $4.50.

Cauer, P., Delectus Inscriptionum Græcarum. 2d ed. 8°. Leip. 1883. 7 M.

Smyth, H. W., The Sounds and Inflections of the Greek Dialects. vol. I. Ionic. Macm. 1894. $6.00.

Kirchhoff, A., Studien zur Geschichte des gr. Alphabets. 4th ed. 8° Gütersloh. 1887. 6 M.

Kuehner, R., Ausführliche Grammatik der lateinischen Sprache. 2 vols. 8°. Leipzig. 1877-79. 25 M.

Roby, H. J., A Grammar of the Lat. Language. 5th ed. 2 vols. 8°. Macm. 1882-7. $4.50.

Madvig, J. N., Lat. Grammar. tr. Thatcher. 8°. B. Ginn. 1880. $2.40.

Hale, W. G., Syntax of the Latin Moods and Tenses. 8°. B. Ginn. $1.50. (*in press*).

Neue, F., Formenlehre der lat. Sprache. 3d ed. 8°. Berlin. 1884+. 32+ M. Vols. I. *and* III. *not yet revised.*

Lindsay, W. M., The Latin Language. 8°. Macm. 1894. $5.00.

Hale, W. G., The "Cum" Constructions: their History and Functions, (*forms vol. I of Cornell studies in Class. Ph.*) 8°. B. Ginn. 1887-89. $1.20. Same is tr. into German by A. Neitzert, with preface by B. Delbrück, rev. and supplemented by the author. 8°. Leipzig. 1891. 6 M.

Potts, ⬥ W., Hints towards Latin Prose Composition. 12°. Macm. 1886. $ .75.

Krebs, J. Th., Antibarbarus der lat. Sprache. 6th ed. rev. Schmalz. 2 vols. 1886-88. 24 M. b.

Peck, H. T., The Pronunciation of Latin. 12°. N. Y. Holt. 1890. $ .40.

Brambach, W., Aids to Lat. Orthography. tr. W. G. McCabe. 16°. Harper. 1877. $1.00.

**Platner, S. B., Greek and Roman Versification. B. Allyn & B. 1892. $ .75.

*Doederlein, L., Handbook of Lat. Synonyms. tr. Arnold and Taylor. 8°. L. Draper. 1875. $1.25.

**Allen, F. D., Remnants of Early Latin. 16°. B. Ginn. 1880. $ .80.

Wordsworth, J., Fragments and Specimens of Early Lat. 8°. Macm. 1874. $4.50.

Rushforth, G. M., Latin Historical Inscriptions. 8°. Macm. 1893. $3.00.

*Wilmanns, G., Exempla Inscriptionum Latinarum. 2 vols. 8°. Berlin. 1873. 20 M.

Dessau, H., Inscriptiones Latinæ Selectæ. vol. I. Berlin. 1892. 11 M.

*Thompson, E. M., Gk. and Lat. Palæography. 8°. App. 1893. $2.00.

Wattenbach, W., Anleitung zur lat. Paläographie. 4th ed. 8°. Leipzig. 1886. 3.60 M.

Wattenbach, W., Anleitung zur gr. Paläographie. 2d ed. 8°. Leip. 1877. 3.60 M.

III. GREEK AND LATIN LITERATURE.

Butcher, S. H., Aristotle's Theory of Poetry and the Fine Arts. 8°. Macm. 1885. $3.50. (Contains text and transl. of Aristotle's Poetics).

Arnold, M., On Translating Homer. In vol. II of Complete Works. 8°. Macm. $1.50.

**Moulton, R. G., The Ancient Classical Drama. 8°. Macm. 1890. $2.25.

Schlegel, A. W. von., Lectures on Dramatic Art and Literature. tr. A. J. W. Morrison. 8°. Macm. 1876. $1.00.

Church, A. J., Stories from 1) *Homer. 2) *Vergil. 3) *Gk. Tragedians. 4) Livy. 5) Pliny. 6) Lucian. 8°. N. Y. Dodd, Mead & Co. $1.00 each.

a. Greek Literature.

A. General Histories and Works on Particular Authors and Subjects.

Mure, W., A Critical History of the Language and Literature of Ancient Greece. 2d ed. 5 vols. 8°. Long. 1854–60. 69s.

Mueller, K. O., and Donaldson, J. W., History of the Literature of Ancient Greece. 3 vols. 8°. L. J. Parker & Co. 1850–58. 36s.

*Mahaffy, J. P., History of Classical Greek Literature. 2 vols. Macm. 1885. $2.25 each.

Perry, T. S., History of Gk. Literature. 8°. Holt. 1890. $7.50.

**Jevons, F. B., History of Greek Literature. 8°. Scribner. 1886. $2.50.

**Jebb, R. C., Greek Literature. 16°. Am. Book Co. 1888. $.35.

Ancient Classics for English Readers. ed. by W. L. Collins. 16°. 28 vols. in 9. Philadelphia. J. B. Lippincott Co. $6.75. The Greek authors treated are:

Homer's Iliad. Homer's Odyssey. Herodotus. Æschylus. Xenophon. Sophocles. Euripides. Aristophanes. Hesiod and Theognis. Greek Anthology. Plato. Lucian. Demosthenes. Aristotle. Thucydides. Pindar. (*Each vol. is also sold separately.*)

**Jebb, R. C., Introduction to Homer. 12°. B. Ginn. 1887. $1.25.

*Clerke, Agnes M., Familiar Studies in Homer. 8°. Long. 1892. $1.75.

*Bonitz, H., Origin of the Homeric Poems. tr. 16°. Harper. 1880. $.75.

*Lang, A., Homer and the Epic. 8°. Long. 1893. $2.25.

Campbell, L., A Guide to Greek Tragedy. 8°. L. Rivington. 1891. 6s.

De Quincey, Thos., Theory of Greek Tragedy. In vol. X. of Collected Writings. 8°. Macm. 1890. $1.25.

**Haigh, A. E., The Attic Theatre. 8°. Macm. 1889. $3.00.

*Jebb, R. C., The Growth and Influence of Classical Greek Poetry. 12°. Houghton, Mifflin & Co. 1893. $1.50.

*Symonds, J. A., Studies in the Greek Poets. 2 vols. 12°. 3d ed. rev. Macm. 1893. $6.00.

De Quincey, Thos., The Philosophy of Herodotus. In vol. V. of Collected Writings. Macm. 1889. $1.25.

*Jebb, R. C., The Attic Orators from Antiphon to Isæus. 2d ed. 2 vols. 8°. Macm. 1893. $5.00.

DeWitte, C., The Retreat of the Ten Thousand. Long. 1891. $1.25.

B. Editions and Translations of Greek Authors.

(Note.—*After line 1 on page 9 add:* " Herodotus. tr. Rawlinson. 4 vols. 8°. App. 1859–60. $8.00.)

**Homer, Iliad. ed. Walter Leaf. (*Eng. notes.*) 2 vols. 8°. Macm. 1888. $4.00.

**Odyssey. ed. Merry and Riddell. (*Eng. notes.*) Bks. I.–XII. (*all now published.*) 2d ed. Macm. 1886. $4.00.

**Hymns. erläutert von A. Gemoll. 8°. Leipzig. 1886. 6.80 M.

Iliad and Odyssey. tr. by (1) Worsley. (2) Chapman. (3) Pope.(4) Bryant.

**Iliad. tr. by (1) Lang, Leaf and Myers (prose). (2) Lord Derby.

**Odyssey. tr. by Butcher and Lang (prose).

**Odyssey. tr. by G. H. Palmer (prose).

Hymns. tr. by (1) P. B. Shelley. In Globe ed. of his Works. 8°. Macm. 1890. $1.75. (2) Edgar.

Cyclic Poets. Corpus Poetarum Epic. Græcorum. vol. I. ed. Kinkel. 8°. Leipzig. 1877. 3 M.

Hesiod. ed. F. A. Paley. (*Eng. notes.*) 2d ed. 8°. Macm. 1883. $1.75.

Anthologia Lyrica. ed. Bergk–Hiller. 8°. Leipzig. 1890. 3 M.

*Æschylus. ed. F. A. Paley. (*Eng. notes.*) 4th ed. 8°. Macm. 1879. $2.75.

tr. E. H. Plumptre. 3d. ed. 16°. L. Strahan & Co. 1873.

*Sophocles. ed. L. Campbell. (*Eng. notes.*) vol. I. 2d ed. 1872. vol. II. 1881. Macm. $4.00 *each.*

tr. E. H. Plumptre. 16°. Routledge. 1882. $1.50.

*Pindar. ed. C. A. M. Fennell. (*Eng. notes.*) 8°. Macm. vol. I. 2d ed. 1893; vol. II. 1883. $4.75.

tr. E. Myers, 8°. Macm. 1874. $1.50.

*Aristophanes. ed. H. Holden. (*Eng. notes.*) 8°. Macm. 1868. $5.00

*Theocritus. ed. Fritsche–Hiller. 3d ed. (*Ger. notes.*) Leipzig. 2.70 M.

*Theocritus, Bion and Moschus. rendered into English prose by A. Lang. 16°. Macm. 1889. $1.00.

Herodotus. ed. J. W. Blakesley. (*Eng. notes.*) 2 vols. Macm. 1854. $4.50.

**Thucydides. In Ginn's College Series of Greek Authors (*incomplete*). ed. Klassen-Steup. 8 vols. 8°. Berlin. 1889. (Steup's *revision is incomplete, it will cost complete about* 20 M.)
  *tr. and annotated by B. Jowett. 2 vols. 8°. Macm. 1881. $8.00.

**Xenophon. ed. Hug, Keller and Dindorf. 8°. Leip. 1875–90. 4.95 M.

**Xenophon. tr. by H. G. Dakyns. 4 vols. 8°. Macm. vols. I. and II. $5.00; vols. III. and IV. *not yet published*.

**Plato. ed. C. F. Hermann and M. Wohlrab. 6 vols. 8°. Leip. 1873–89. 10.50 M.

**Plato, Dialogues. tr. by B. Jowett. 3d ed. 4 vols. 8°. Macm. 1892. $20.00.

*Euripides. ed. F. A. Paley. (*Eng. notes.*) 2d ed. 3 vols. 8°. L. Whittaker & Co. 1889. 8s. *each.*
  tr. A. S. Way. 3 vols. 8°. Macm. vol. I. 1894. $2.00. vols. II. and III. *not yet published.*

Oratores Attici:
  Antiphon. ed. F. Blass. 8°. Leip. 1881. 2.10 M.
  Andocides. ed. F. Blass. 8°. Leip. 1880. 1.20 M.
  Lysias. ed. C. Scheibe. 8°. Leip. 1882. 1.20 M.
  Isocrates. ed. Benseler-Blass. 2 vols. 8°. Leip. 1888–9. 2.70 M.
  Isaeus. ed. C. Scheibe. 8°. Leip. 1875. 1.20 M.
  *Demosthenes. ed. Dindorf-Blass. 4th ed. 3 vols. 8°. Leip. 1885–89. 7.20 M.
  Aeschines. ed. F. Franke. 8°. Leip. 1873. .90 M.
  Lycurgus. ed. C. Scheibe. 8°. Leip. 1871. .60 M.
  Hyperides. ed. F. Blass. 8°. Leip. 1888. 1.00 M.
  Dinarchus. ed. F. Blass. 2d ed. 8°. Leip. 1881. 1.35 M.

*Aristotle, Opera Omnia. (*Crit. ap.*) 5 vols. 8°. Firmin Didot. Paris. 1848–74. 80 Francs.

*Politics. tr. by Welldon. 12°. Macm. 1883. $2.50.
Ethics. tr. by T. H. Peters. 3d ed. 8°. L. Keagan Paul, Trench, Trübner & Co. 1881. 6s.
Rhetoric. tr. by Welldon. 16°. Macm. 1886. $2.00.
Politeia Athenaiōn. ed. E. Sandys.(*Eng. notes.*) 8°. Macm. 1893. $3.75.
*Polybius. ed. F. Hultsch. 4 vols. 8°. Berlin. 1872–92. 16.50 M.
Dionysius of Halicarnassus. ed. C. Jacoby. 4 vols. Leip. vols. I.-III. 9.60 M. IV. *in press.*
Diodorus Siculus. ed. Dindorf-Vogel. 5 vols. 8°. Leip. 1867–93. 19.95 M.
[Longinus], On the Sublime. tr. by H. L. Havell. 8°. Macm. 1890. $1.10.
*Plutarch, Vitae Parallelae. ed. C. Sintenis. 5 vols. 8°. Leip. 1873–75. 8.40. M.
Moralia. recog. G. N. Bernardakis. 5 vols. 8°. Leip. 1889–94. 15 M.
**Lives. tr. by Dryden-Clough. 8°. Little, B. & Co. 1888. $2.00.
Morals. tr. by various hands. 5 vols. 8°. Little, B. & Co. 1874. $15.00.
Strabo. ed. Meineke. 3 vols. Leip. 1866. 6 M.
Josephus. tr. Shilleto. 5 vols. 12°. L. Bell. 1889–90. $5.00.

Dio Cassius. ed. Dindorf-Melber. 5 vols. 8°. Leip. 1890+. vols. III.-V.
not yet revised. 8.60+ M.

New Testament in the Original Greek. ed. B. F. Westcott & F. J. A.
Hort. 8°. 2 vols. Harper. 1881. $4.00.

Epictetus. tr. Geo. Long. 8°. Macm. 1877. $1.50.

*Pausanias. ed. Schubart. 2 vols. 8°. Leip. 1875. 3.60 M.

*Pausanias. tr. by Shilleto. 2 vols. 8°. Macm. 1886. $1.50 *each.*

Arrian. ed. C. Abicht and R. Hercher. 2 vols. 8°. Leip. 1875-86. 3.30 M.

Arrian. tr. E. J. Chinnock. 8°. Macm. 1893. $1.50.

Lucian. ed. Sommerbrodt. (*Crit. ap.*) 8°. Berlin. 1886+. 15+ M.

Marcus Aurelius, Meditations. tr. by Geo. Long. 7th ed. 8°. Little, B.
& Co. 1889. $1.50.

Diogenes Laertius. tr. C. D. Yonge. 8°. Macm. 1853. $1.50.

b. Latin Literature.

A. General Histories and Works on Particular Authors and Subjects.

Teuffel, W. S., A History of R. Literature. tr. G. C. W. Warr. 2 vols. 8°.
Macm. $4.00 *each.*

Simcox, G. A., A History of L. Literature. 2 vols. 12°. Harper. 1883. $4.00.

Cruttwell, C. T., A History of Roman Literature. 2d ed. 8°. Scribner.
1888. $2.50.

Dunlop, John, History of Roman Literature. 3 vols. 8°. Long. 1824-28.

Bender, H., A Brief History of R. Literature. tr. 2d ed. Ginn. 1880. $1.00.

Kelsey, F. W., Topical Outline of Latin Literature. 12°. B. Allyn &
B. 1891. $ .35. (*Bibliographical.*)

Harrington, K. P., Helps to the Intelligent Study of College Preparatory
Latin. Ginn. 1888. $ .35. (*Bibliographical.*)

Ancient Classics for English Readers. ed. W. L. Collins. 16°. 28 vols.
in 9. Lippincott. $6.75. includes: Cæsar. Vergil. Horace. Cicero.
Pliny's Letters. Juvenal. Plautus and Terence. Tacitus. Livy.
Ovid. Catullus. Lucretius. (*Each vol. is also sold separately.*)

Tyrrell, R. Y., Latin Poetry. 8°. H., M. & Co. 1895. $1.50.

Sellar, W. Y., The R. Poets of the Republic. 3d ed. 8°. Macm. 1889. $2.50.

Newman, J. H., Cicero. In vol. I. of Hist. Sketches. 8°. Long. 1891. $1.25.

*Forsyth, W., Life of Marcus Tullius Cicero. 1 vol. Scribner. 1877. $2.50.

Faussett, W. Y., The Student's Cicero. 8°. Macm. 1890. $1.00.

De Quincey, Thos., Cicero. In vol. VI. of Collected Writings. Macm.
1889-90. $1.25.

Trollope, A., The Life of Cicero. 2 vols. 8°. Harper. 1881. $3.00.

Dodge, T. A., Cæsar. 8°. H., M. & Co. 1892. $5.00.

*Froude, J. A., Cæsar: A Sketch. 8°. N. Y. Scribner. 1879. $1.50.

Napoleon III., History of Julius Cæsar. tr. 2 vols. and atlas. 8°. Harper.
1865-66. $7.00. cheap ed. $4.00.

*Goeler, A. von, Cæsars Gallische Kriege. 8°. Freiburg. 1880. 18 M.

Heynacher, M., Sprachgebrauch Cæsars. 2d ed. 8°. Berlin. 1886. 3 M.

Lupus, B., Der Sprachgebrauch des C. Nepos. 8°. Berlin. 1876. 6.40 M.

Sellar, W. Y., The Roman Poets of the Augustan Age, Vergil. 2d ed. 8°.
Macm. 1883. $2.25.

Nettleship, H., Ancient Lives of Vergil. 8°. Macm. 1879. $ .50.

Tunison, J. S., Master Virgil. 2d ed. 8°. Cincinnati. Robert Clarke & Co. 1888. $2.00.

**Sellar, W. Y., The Roman Poets of the Augustan Age, Horace, etc. 8°. Macm. 1892. $3.50.

Conington, J., Miscellaneous Essays. vol. I. 8°. Long. 1872. 14s.

*Nettleship, H., Lectures and Essays. 8°. Macm. 1885. $1.90.

B. Editions and Translations of Latin Authors.

**Plautus. rec. Goetz and Schoell. 12°. Leip. 1893+. 2.70+ M. *small ed.*

**Terence. rec. C. Dziatzko. 8°. Leipzig. 1884. 1.20 M.

Cato, M. Porcius. ed. Keil. vol. I. part 1. 8°. Leipzig. 1882. 2.40 M.

Varro, De Re Rustica. ed. Keil. 8°. Leipzig. 1889. 1.50 M.

**Cicero, Opera. rec. Baiter et Kayser. 11 vols. 8°. Leip. 1860–69. 21.75 M.

Letters. ed. R. Y. Tyrrell. (*Eng. notes.*) 4 vols. 8°. Long. 1885–95. vol. I. to III. $3.80 *each*, vol. IV. $4.25.

Epistolæ. ed. L. Mendelssohn. (*Crit. Ap.*) 8°. Leip. 1893. 12 M.

Orations. ed. Geo. Long. (*Eng. notes.*) 4 vols. 8°. Macm. 1855–62. vol. I. and II. $2.75 *each*. vols. III. and IV. *out of print*.

**Nepos, Vitæ. rec. Fleckeisen. 8°. Leipzig. 1884. .30 M.

**Cæsar, Commentarii cum Hirtii aliorumque supplementis. ed. Kübler. (*Crit. ap.*) 2 vols. 8°. Leip. 1893–94. 2.10 M.

De Bello Gallico. ed. Meusel. 8°. Berlin. 1894. 4 M. b.

De Bello Gallico. ed. Moberly. (*Eng. notes.*) 16°. Macm. $2.25.

ed. Peskett. (*Eng. notes.*) 5 vols. 16°. Macm. $2.55.

erklärt Fr. Kraner. (*Ger. notes.*) 15th ed. Berlin. 1890. 2.25 M.

De Bello Civili. ed. Moberly. (*Eng. notes.*) 16°. Macm. 1880. $1.50.

ed. Peskett. (*Eng. notes.*) 16°. Macm. 1890+ $.80+

De Bello Civili. erklärt Kraner and Hoffmann. (*Ger. notes*). 10th ed. 8°. Berlin. 1890. $2.25. M.

**Lucretius. ed. Munro. (*Eng. notes.*) 3 vols. 8°. Macm. 1886. $6.00.

**Sallust. ed. Dietsch. 8°. Leipzig. 1887. .45 M.

*Catullus. ed. Merrill. (*Eng. notes.*) 12°. B. Ginn. 1893. $1.50.

**Vergil. ed. Conington and Nettleship. (*Eng. notes.*) 3 vols. 8°. Macm. 1872–75. $9.75.

ed. Papillon and Haigh. (*Eng. notes.*) 2 vols. 8°. Macm. 1892. $2.75.

ed. Heyne–Wagner. (*Crit. ap.*) 4th ed. 5 vols. 8°. Hannover. 1830–41. 60 M.

tr. Conington. In vol. II. of Miscellaneous Essays. 14s.

**Horace. ed. Wickham. (*Eng. notes.*) 2 vols. 8°. Macm. 1877–91. $6.00.

*Tibullus. ed. Hiller. 8°. Leipzig. 1885. .60 M.

*Propertius. ed. Palmer. (*Eng. notes.*) 8°. Macm 1880. $1.25.

**Ovid. ed. Riese. 3 vols. 8°. Leipsic. 1871–74. 8.40 M.

**Livius. ed. Weissenborn. 6 vols. 8°. Leipzig. 1887. 6 M.

*Livius. Book I. ed. Seeley. (*Eng. notes.*) 3d ed. 8°. Macm. 1881. $1.50.

Iustinus. ed. Jepp. 8°. Leipzig. 1886. 1.50 M.

Seneca, M. Annæus. ed. Kiessling. 8°. Leipzig. 1872. 4.50 M.

Velleius Paterculus. ed. Halm. 8°. Leipzig. 1876. 1 M.

Valerius Maximus. ed. Kempf. 8°. Leipzig. 1889. 4.50 M.

Phædrus. ed. L. Müller. 8°. Leipzig. 1888. .30 M.

Seneca, L. Annæus, Opera. ed. Haase. 3 vols. Leipzig. 1872–74. 7.80 M.

tragœdiæ. ed. Peiper and Richter. 8°. Leipzig. 1867. 4.50 M.

*Curtius. ed. Vogel. 8°. Leip. 1880. 1.20 M.

*Persius. ed. Conington and Nettleship. (*Eng. notes.*) 8°. Macm. 1893. $2.25.

Lucan. ed. Haskins and Heitland. (*Eng. notes.*) 8°. L. Bell. 1887. 14s.

*Pliny, Hist. Nat. ed. Jahn–Mayhoff. 6 vols. 8°. Leipzig. 1892. 14.40 M.

Valerius Flaccus. ed. Baehrens. 8°. Leipzig. 1875. 1.50 M.

Statius. ed. Baehrens and Kohlmann. 8°. Leipzig. 1876–84. 7.35 M.

Silius Italicus. ed. Bauer. 2 vols. 8°. Leipzig. 1890–92. 4.80 M.

*Martial. ed. Gilbert. 8°. Leipzig. 1886. 2.40 M.

*Quintilian, Institutiones. ed. F. Meissner 2 vols. 8°. Prague. 1887. 2.70 M.

Declamationes. ed. Ritter. 8°. 1884. 4.80 M.

*Juvenal. ed. Mayor. (*Eng notes.*) 4th ed. 2 vols. 8°. Macm. 1888–93. $4.00

**Tacitus. ed. Halm. 2 vols. 8°. Leipzig. 1883–93. 3.90 M.

Annals. ed. Furneaux. (*Eng. notes.*) 8°. Macm. 1882. $4.00.

Histories. ed. Spooner. (*Eng. notes.*) 8°. Macm. 1891. $3.50.

Dialogus. ed. Gudeman, A. (*Eng. notes.*) 8°. B. Ginn. 1894. $3.00.

*Pliny, Epistulæ. ed. Keil. 8°. Leipzig. 1873. 1.20 M.

Suetonius. ed. Roth. 1 vol. 8°. Leipzig. 1875. 1.50 M.

Gellius. ed. Hertz. 2 vols. 8°. Leipzig. 1886. 4.20 M.

Florus. ed. Halm. 8°. Leipzig. 1879. 1 M.

Fronto. ed. Naber. (*Crit. ap.*) 8°. Leipzig. 1867. 8 M.

Eutropius. ed. Ruehl. 8°. Leipzig. 1887. .45 M.

Servius. ed. Thilo and Hagen. (*Crit. ap.*) 3 vols. 8°. Leipzig. 1878–94. 54.50 M.

Macrobius. ed. Eyssenhardt. 8°. Leipzig. 1893. 6 M.

Scriptores Historiæ Augustæ. rec. Peter. 8°. Leipzig. 1884. 7.50 M.

Poetae Latini Minores. ed. Baehrens. 5 vols. Leip. 1879–83. 15.90 M.

IV. RELIGION AND MYTHOLOGY.

Roscher, W. H., Lexicon der griechischen und römischen Mythologie. 8°. Leipzig. 1890+. 36+ M. (*now publishing.*)

*Lang, A.**, Myth, Ritual, and Religion. 2 vols. 8°. Long. 1887. 21s.

Fiske, John, Myths and Myth-Makers. 8°. J. R. Osgood & Co. (H., M. & Co.) 1874. $2.00.

Frazer, T. G., The Golden Bough. 2 vols. 8°. Macm. 1890. $5.00.

Murray, A. S., Manual of Mythology. 2d ed. 8°. Scribner. 1888. $1.75.

Collignon, M., Manual of Mythology. tr. by J. E. Harrison. 8°. L. Grevel & Co. 1890. 10s. 6d.

*Gayley, C. M.**, Classic Myths in English Literature. 2d ed. B. Ginn. 1895. $1.65.

*Bulfinch, T.**, The Age of Fable. rev. ed. 12°. Lee & Shepard. 1894. $2.50.

Kingsley, C., The Heroes. rev. ed. 8°. Macm. 1888. $1.25.

Coulanges, Fustel de, The Ancient City. 3d ed. 12°. Lee & S. 1873. $1.60.

Dyer, L., The Gods of Greece. 12°. Macm. 1894. $2.00.

V. PUBLIC AFFAIRS.

a. Geography.

Freeman, E. A., Historical Geography of Europe. 2 vols. 8°. Long. 1881. $10.50.

Tozer, H. F., Classical Geography. 16°. Am. Bk. Co. 1878. $ .35.

*Desjardins, E., Geographie de la Gaule romaine. 4 vols. 4°. Libraire Hachette. 1876-93. 78 Fr.

Mahaffy, J. P., Greek Pictures. N. Y. F. H. Revell & Co. 1890. $3.20.

Freeman, E. A., Studies of Travel. vol. I. Greece. vol. II. Italy. 8°. Putnam. 1893. $1.50.

Tozer, H. F., Islands of the Aegean. 12°. Macm. 1890. $2.25.

b. History and Chronology.

A. Eastern.

Putnams' 'Stories of the Nations' Series. N. Y. G. P. Putnam's Sons. The following volumes at $1.50 per volume :

The Story of Persia. By S. G. W. Benjamin.
"   "   " Phoenicia. By Geo. Rawlinson.
"   "   " the Jews under Rome. By W. Douglas.
"   "   " Ancient Egypt. By Geo. Rawlinson.

B. Greece.

(For legendary history see also under Homer in Class *III, a*.)
'Stories of the Nations,' the following volumes :

The Story of Alexander's Empire. By J. P. Mahaffy and A. Gilman.
"   "   " Sicily. By E. A. Freeman.
"   "   " the Byzantine Empire. By C. W. C. Oman.

**Grote, Geo., History of Greece. 10 vols. 8°. Little. B. & Co. 1888. $17.50.

**Curtius, E., History of Greece. tr. by Ward and Packard. 5 vols. 8°. Scribner. 1888. $10.00.

Duruy, V., History of Greece and of the Greek People to 146 B. C. 8 vols. 8°. L. Keagan Paul. 1891. £8 8s.

Ranke, L. von, Universal History. vol. I. ed. G. W. Prothero. 8°. Harper. 1885. $2.50.

Holm, A., History of Greece to [146 B. C.] vol. I. [*all that is published*] 12°. Macm. 1894. $2.50.

Oman, C. W. C., History of Greece to 323 B. C. 8°. Long. 1892. $1.50.

Cox, G. W., The Greeks and the Persians. 12°. Scribner. 1876. $1.00.

*Lloyd, W. W., The Age of Pericles. 2 vols. 8°. Macm. 1875. $8.00.

Cox, G. W., The Athenian Empire. 12°. Scribner. 1876. $1.00.

Grote, Geo., Two Great Retreats of History. 12°. B. Ginn. 1889. $ .50.

Sankey, C., The Spartan and Theban Supremacies. 12°. Long. 1886. $1.00.

Dodge, T. A., Alexander. 8°. H., M. & Co. 1890. $5.00.

Freeman, E. A., Chief Periods of European History. 8°. Macm. 1886. $2.50.

Mahaffy, J. P., The Greek World under Roman Sway. From Polybius to Plutarch. 12°. Macm. 1890. $3.00.

*Freeman, E. A., The History of Sicily. 4 vols. Macm. 1891-95. $21.50.

Freeman, E. A., Greater Greece and Greater Britain. 8°. Macm. 1886. $1.00.

Freeman, E. A., History of Federal Government in Greece and Italy. 8°. Macm. 1893. $3.75.

Felton, C. C., Greece, Anc. and Mod. new ed. H., M. & Co. 1886. $5.00.

**Gardner, P., New Chapters in Greek History. 8°. Putnam. 1892. $5.00.

Mahaffy, J. P., Problems in Greek History. 12°. Macm. 1892. $2.50.

C. Rome.

De Quincey, Thos., The Philosophy of Roman History. In vol. VI. of his Works. 8°. Macm. 1889-90. $1.25.

Tighe, A., The Roman Constitution. 16°. Am. Book Co. 1886. $ .35.

**Duruy, V., History of Rome and the Roman People. tr. by Clarke and Ripley. 6 vols. Estes and Lauriat. 1883-86. $6.00 each.

Merivale, Charles, A General History of Rome. 8°. Long. 1875. $2.00.

Pelham, H. F., Outlines of Roman History. Putnam. 1893. $1.75.

Gilman, A., The Story of Rome. Putnam. 1885. $1.50

**Mommsen, Th., The History of Rome. new ed. 4 vols. 8°. Scribner. 1887. $6.00.

Liddell, H. S., History of Rome. 12°. Harper. 1863. $1.25.

Arnold, Thos., History of Rome to 241 B. C. 5th ed. L. H. Bickers & Son. 1882. 24s.

Ihne, Wm., History of Rome. 5 vols. Long. 1871-82. 77s.

Ihne, Wm., Early Rome. 4th ed. Scribner. 1886. $1 00.

Arnold, T., The Second Punic War. 8°. Macm. 1886. $2.25.

Smith, R. Bosworth., Rome and Carthage. 8°. Long. 1881. $1.00.

Church, A. J., The Story of Carthage. 8°. Putnam. $1.50.

Dodge, T. A., Hannibal. 8°. H., M. & Co. 1891. $5.00.

Long, Geo., Decline of the R. Republic. 5 vols. 8°. Macm. 1864-67. $7.50.

Beesly, A. H., The Gracchi, Marius and Sulla. 8°. Long. 1886. $1.00.

*Merivale, C., The Fall of the R. Republic. 2d ed. 8°. Long. 1853. $2.25.

Merivale, C., The Roman Triumvirates. 8°. Long. 1876. $1.00.

Forsyth, Wm., Hortensius, the Advocate. 3d ed. 8°. L. J. Murray. 1879. 7s. 6d.

*Davidson, J. L. S., Cicero and the Fall of the Roman Republic. 8°. Putnam. 1894. $1.50.

**Fowler, W. W., Julius Cæsar and the Organization of the Roman Empire. 8°. Putnam. 1892. $1.50.

*Merivale, C., History of the Romans under the Empire. 8 vols. 8°. Long. 1890. $10.00.

Capes, W. W., The Early Empire. 6th ed. Long. 1887. $1.00.

De Quincey, Thos., The Cæsars. In vol. VI. of his Works. 8°. Macm. 1889-90. $1.25.

Capes, W. W., The Age of the Antonines. 8°. Long. 1887. $1.00.

**Gibbon, Edward, History of the Decline and Fall of the Roman Empire. 6 vols. 8°. Harper. 1880. $12 00.

Sheppard, J. G., The Fall of Rome. 12°. N. Y. Geo. Routledge & Sons. 1894. $1.50.

*Bryce, J., The Holy Roman Empire. 8th ed. 8°. Macm. 1889. $3.50.

Emerton, E., An Introduction to the Study of the Middle Ages. 8°. B. Ginn. 1888. $1.25.

Emerton. E., Mediæval Europe. 12°. B. Ginn. 1894. $1.65.

Hodgkin, T., Italy and Her Invaders. 4 vols. 8°. Macm. 1883–85. $21.50.

*Bury, J. B., History of the Later R. Empire. 2 vols. 8°. Macm. 1889. $8.00.

Bury, J. B., History of the Roman Empire. 12°. Harper. 1893. $1.50.

Seeley, J. R., Roman Imperialism. In his Lectures and Essays. 16°. B. Roberts Bros. 1871. $1.00.

Bradley, H., The Story of the Goths. Putnam. 1888. $1.50.

Scarth, H. M., Roman Britain. 12°. L. Society for the Promotion of Christian Knowledge. 1883. 2s. 6d.

Wright, T., The Celt, the Roman, and the Saxon. 4th ed. 8°. Trübner. (Keagan Paul). 1885. 9s.

*Ranke, L. von, History of the Latin and Teutonic Nations. tr. 8°. Little, B. & Co. 1887. $1.40.

Kingsley, C., The Roman and the Teuton. 8°. Macm. 1889. $1.25.

Arnold, Thos., The Roman System of Provincial Administration. 8°. Macm. 1879. (out of print.)

*Mommsen, Th., The Provinces of the Roman Empire from Cæsar to Diocletian. 2 vols. 8°. Scribner. 1887. $6.00.

Milman, H. H., History of Christianity to the Abolition of Paganism. 3 vols. 8°. Also History of Later Christianity. 4 vols. 8°. Scribner. 1883. $10.50.

c. Political Antiquities.

*Fowler, W. W., City-State of the Greeks and Romans. 16°. Macm. 1893. $1.00.

Morey, W. C., Outlines of Roman Law. 6th ed. 8°. Putnam. 1892. $1.75.

**Boeckh, A., Public Economy of the Athenians tr. by A. Lamb. 8°. Little, B. & Co. 1857.

Schoemann, G. F., Antiquities of Greece. tr. by Hardy and Mann. 8°. Rivington. 1880. 10s.

**Judson, H. P., Caesar's Army. 12°. B. Ginn. 1888. $1.10.

VI. PRIVATE AFFAIRS.

Compayré, G., History of Pedagogy. 8°. D. C. Heath & Co. 1886. $1.75.

Davidson, T., Aristotle and Ancient Educational Ideals. 8°. Scribner. 1892. $1.00.

Mahaffy, J. P., Old Greek Education. 24°. Harper. 1882. $.75.

Capes, W. W., University Life in Ancient Athens. 32". Harper. 1877. $.25.

Inge, W. R., Society in R. under the Caesars. 8°. Scribner. 1888. $1.25.

Church, A. J., Roman Life in the Days of Cicero. N. Y. Dodd. 1884. $1.00.

*Bluemner, H., Home Life of the Ancient Greeks. tr. by A. Zimmern. N. Y. Cassell Pub. Co. 1893. $2.00.

Church, A. J., Pictures from Roman Life and Story. 8°. App. 1892.

*Preston and Dodge, Private Life of the Romans. 8°. L., S. & S. 1894. $1.00.

Evans, M. M., Chapters on Greek Dress. 8°. Macm. 1893. $2.00.

VII. FINE ARTS.

a. Histories of the Arts.

Luebke, W., Outlines of the History of Art. tr. by C. Cook. 2 vols. large 8°. N. Y. Dodd. 1887, $14.00.

*****Winckelmann, J.**, The History of Ancient Art. tr. by G. H. Lodge. 2 vols. 8°. B. Osgood. (H., M. & Co.) 1880. $9.00.

Reber, F. von, A History of Ancient Art. tr. by J. T. Clarke. 8°. Harper. 1883. $3.50.

*****Luebke, W.**, A History of Sculpture. tr. by F. E. Bennett. 2 vols. large 8°. Lipp. 1872. $18.00.

****Mitchell, Lucy M.**, A History of Ancient Sculpture. 4°. N. Y. Dodd. 1883. $12.50. *cheap ed.* 1888. $7.50.

Murray, A. S., History of Gk. Sculpture. 2 vols. 8°. Scribner. 1884. $14.00.

Perry, W. C., Greek and Roman Sculpture. 8°. Scribner. 1882. $12.00.

*****Paris, P.**, Manual of Ancient Sculpture. ed. by J. E. Harrison. Lipp. 1890. $3.00.

Upcott, L. E., An Introduction to Greek Sculpture. 8°. Macm. 1887. $1.10.

****Harrison, E. J.**, Introductory Studies in Gk. Art. 8°. Macm. 1892. $2.25.

Perrot and Chipiez, History of Art in Primitive Greece. 2 vols. 4°. L. Chapman & Hall. 1894. $15.50.

Furtwaengler, A., Masterpieces of Greek Sculpture. tr. by E. Sellers. 4°. Scribner. 1895. $15.00.

Waldstein, C., Essays on the Art of Pheidias. 8°. Century Co. 1885. $7.50.

Gardner, P., Types of Greek Coins. 4°. Macm. 1883. $8.00.

Woltmann, A., and Woermann, K., History of Painting. tr. by C. Bell. 2 vols. 4°. N. Y. Dodd. 1886-88. *cheap ed.* $7.50.

Fergusson, J., A History of Architecture. vols. I. and II. Little, B. & Co. 1874. 63s.

Durm, T., Die Baukunst der Griechen. 2d ed. 8°. Darmstadt. 1892. 20 M.

Jacquemart, A., History of the Ceramic Art. tr. by Mrs. Palliser. 2d ed. 8°. Scribner. 1877. $10.50.

Monro, D. B., Modes of Ancient Greek Music. 8°. Macm. $2.50.

b. Descriptive Handbooks, etc., of Archaeology and Art.

Baumeister, A., Denkmäler des klassischen Altertums. 3 vols. 4°. Munich. 1885-88. *can be bought for about* 45 M.

Baedeker, K., Italy. Pt. I. Northern Italy. 9th ed. Leip. 1892. 8 M.

　Pt. II. Central Italy and Rome. 10th ed. Leip. 1890. 6 M.

　Pt. III. Southern Italy. 10th ed. Leip. 1890. 6 M.

****Middleton, J. H.**, Remains of Ancient Rome. 2 vols. 8°. Macm. 1892. $7.00.

Burn, R., Ancient Rome and Its Neighborhood. 8°. Macm. 1895. $2.25.

*****Ziegler, C.**, Das alte Rom. 4°. Stuttgart. 1882. 4.50 M.

Shumway, E. S., A Day in Ancient Rome. 12°. Heath. 1887. $ .75. (A translation and revision of Lohr's Aus dem alten Rom.)

**Lanciani, R., Ancient Rome in the Light of Recent Discoveries. 8°. H., M. & Co., 1884. $6.00.
Murray, J., A Handbook of Rome and Its Environs. 14th ed. L. Murray. 1887. 19s.
Hare, A. J. C., Walks in Rome. 11th ed. 1 vol. 12°. Routledge. $3.50.
Hare, A. J. C., Days near Rome. 3d ed. 2 vols. 8°. Routledge. 1884. $5.00.
Taine, H. A., Italy—Naples and Rome. tr. Durand. 8°. Holt. 1875. $2.50.
Lanciani, R., Pagan and Christi in Rome. 8°. II., M. & Co. 1893. $6.00.
Dyer, T. H., Pompeii. 4th ed. 8. Macm. 1891. $2.25.
Ruskin, J., Mornings in Florence. 8. Orpington. Allen. 1883. 4s.
Dennis, G., The Cities and Cemeteries of Etruria. rev. ed. 2 vols. 8°. L. Murray. 1883. 21s.
*Baedeker, K., Greece. 16°. Leip. 1889. 10 M. b.
Harrison, J. E., and **Verrall, A. W., Mythology and Monuments of Ancient Athens. 8°. Macm. 1890. $4.00.
Schliemann, Sellers, Schuchhardt and Leaf. Excavations at Troy, Tiryns, Mycenæ, Orchomenos and Ithaca. 8°. Macm. 1891. $4.00.
Diehl, C., Excursions in Greece. tr. Pool. 8°. Westermann. 1893. $2.00.
Mahaffy, J. P., Rambles and Studies in Greece. 3d ed. Macm. 1887. $3.00.
Dyer, P., Ancient Athens. 8°. L. Bell. 1873. 25s.
**Newton, C. T., Essays on Art and Archaeology. 8°. Macm. 1880. $4.00.
Collignon, M., Handbook of Gk. Archæology. tr. 12°. Cassell. 1886. $2.00.
*Murray, A. S., Handbook of Gk. Archæology. 8°. Scribner. 1892. $5.00.
Burn, A. S., Roman Literature and Roman Art. 8°. Macm. 1889. $2.25.

VIII. PHILOSOPHY AND SCIENCE.

*Zeller, Ed., The Philosophy of the Greeks. new ed. 7 vols. Long. 1877–83.
Vols. i–ii. Pre-Socratic Schools. tr. by S. F. Alleyne. $10.00.
Vol. iii. Socrates and the Socratic Schools. tr. O. J. Reichel. $3.50.
Vol. iv. Plato and the Older Academy. tr. S. F. Alleyne and E. Goodwin. $6.00.
Vol. v. Aristotle and the Elder Peripatetics. tr. T. H. Muirhead. (*not yet published.*)
Vol. vi. Stoics, Epicureans and Sceptics. tr. O. J. Reichel. $5.00.
Vol. vii. History of Eclecticism. tr. S. F. Alleyne. $3.50.
**Zeller, Ed., Outlines of the History of Greek Philosophy. tr. by S. F. Alleyne and E. Abbot. 8°. Holt. 1886. $1.75. (*Epitome of the above.*)
*Ueberweg, Fr., A History of Philosophy. tr. by Geo. S. Morris. vol. I. Ancient and Mediaeval Philosophy. 8°. Scribner. 1889. $2.50.
Burt, B. C., History of Greek Philosophy. 12°. B. Ginn. 1888. $1.25.
Ferrier, T. F., Lectures on Early Greek Philosophy. 4th ed. 2 vols. 8°. L. Wm. Blackwood & Sons. 1882. 14s.
Pater, W., Plato and Platonism. 8°. Macm. 1893. $1.75.
Lewes, G. H., Aristotle, a Chapter from the History of Science. 8°. L. Smith, Elder & Co. 1864. 15s.
Osborn, H. F., From the Greeks to Darwin. 8°. Macm. 1894. $2.00.

IX. MISCELLANEOUS ESSAYS.

*Butcher, S. H., Some Aspects of the Gk. Genius. 12°. Macm 1894. $2.50.
Story, W. W., Excursions in Art and Letters. 12°. H., M. & Co. 1891. $1.25.
Symonds, J. A., Sketches and Studies in Southern Europe. 2 vols. 12°. Harper. 1880. $4.00.
Rydberg, V., Roman Days. tr. Clark. 2d ed. 8°. Putnam. 1887. $2.00.
Myers, F. W., Classical Essays. 1 vol. 12°. Macm. 1888. $1.25.
Abbott, E. A., Hellenica. 8°. Rivington. 1880. 16s.
*Pater, W., Greek Studies. ed. by C. S. Shadwell. 8°. Macm. 1895. $1.75.
Kingsley, C., Historical Lectures and Essays. In vol. XVI. of his Works. 8°. Macm. 1880. $1.25.
*Freeman, E. A., Historical Essays. 2d series. 3d ed. 8°. Macm. $3.00.
Freeman, E. A., Historical and Architectural Sketches. 8°. Macm. 1876. $3.00.
Creasy, E. S., Fifteen Decisive Battles. 12°. Harper. 1872. $1.00.

X. INFLUENCE OF GREECE AND ROME.

Hatch, E., The Influence of Greek Ideas and Usages on the Christian Church. 3d ed. L. Wms. & Norgate. 1891. 10s. 6d.
Renan, E., On the Influence of the Institutions, Thought and Culture of Rome on Christianity. 8°. L. Wms. & Norgate. 1885. 10s. 6d.
*Story, W. W., Roba di Roma. 2 ed. 2 vols. 16°. H., M. & Co. 1887. $2.50.
*Gladstone, W. E., Place of Ancient Greece. In his Gleanings, vol. VII. 16°. Scribner. 1879. $1.00.
*Davidson, T., Education of the Greek People and Its Influence on Civilization. 12°. App. 1894. $1.50.
Symonds, J. A., The Revival of Learning. 8°. Holt. 1882. $3.50.
Voigt, G., Wiederbelebung des klassischen Alterthums. 3d ed. 2 vols. 8°. Berlin. 1894. 18.50 M. b.

XI. ENGLISH NOVELS, ETC., ILLUSTRATING THE LIFE OF CLASSICAL ANTIQUITY.

Chaucer, Arcite and Palemon, Legende of Goode Women; Church, 2000 Years Ago; Ebers, Homo Sum, Serapis, The Emperor; Eckstein, Nero, Prusius, Quintus Claudius, The Chaldean Magician; Herbert, The Roman Traitor; Kingsley, Hypatia; Knowles, Virginius; Landor, Pericles and Aspasia, Imaginary Conversations, Poems; Lockhart, Valerius; Lytton, Last Days of Pompeii; *Macaulay, Lays of Ancient Rome, ed. W. J. and J. C. Rolfe; Newman, Callista; *Pater, Marius the Epicurean; Richardson, The Son of a Star; Shakespeare, Troilus and Cressida and other dramas; Taylor, Antinous; Wallace, Ben-Hur; Ware, Aurelian, Julian, Zenobia; Wiseman, Fabiola; Browning, Cleon, Balaustian's Adventure; Byron, Childe Harold's Pilgrimage; Ebers, The Egyptian Princess; Lang, Helen of Troy, Letters to Dead Authors; Morris, L., The Epic of Hades; Morris, W., Earthly Paradise, Life and Death of Jason; Swinbourne, Atalanta in Calydon.

American Book Company.

NEW BOOKS of this Company are notable for the variety, and in some instances for the novelty of the subjects treated, as well as for the ripe scholarship, professional skill, and school experience that have been employed in their production. They are evidence of the Company's well known policy of keeping abreast of the times and in touch with the best educational thought of the day.

The Company issues the leading American text-books for Common Schools, High Schools, and College Preparatory Schools, books that are in satisfactory use in nearly every country and city school, public and private, in the United States. They possess those subtle, indefinable qualities which cause school books *to wear well.* By careful revision whenever necessary these books are kept constantly fresh and up to date, so that practically they are new books, with the advantage of having stood the test of use.

Orders by mail receive prompt and careful attention; a convenience appreciated by purchasers.

A Bulletin of New Books is sent free on request. Address American Book Company, New York, Cincinnati, Chicago, Boston, or Portland, Ore., whichever is nearest.

GINN & COMPANY,

Publishers of

High School and College Text-Books,

CHICAGO,

355-361 Wabash Avenue.

ATLAS OF CLASSICAL ANTIQUITIES

—BY—

TH. SCHREIBER.

Edited for English use by Prof. W. C. F. Anderson. With a Preface by Prof. Percy Gardner.

Oblong 4to. Cloth, $6.50 net.

Selected Subjects Illustrated and Treated of in the Text of Schreiber's Atlas.

The Drama: The Greek, Roman, and Pompeiian Theatre—Stage Scenes from Plays—Scenes illustrating Classical Costumes— Musical Instruments — Sculpture, Painting, and Casting in Bronze—Metal Work, Painting, and Architecture — Religion (Greek)—Primitive Sanctuaries and Idols—Temples and Sacrifice—Votive Offerings—Mysteries and Various Cults—Altars and Priests—Vestals and Augurs—Races, Games, and Greek Athletics—Roman Amphitheatres, the Colosseum, and Games in the Circus—Charioteers and Gladiators—Greek Armour— Roman Soldiers and Barbarian Armour — Roman Camps and Cavalry — Sieges, Bridges and Ships — Greek and Roman Walls and Gateways—Plans of Houses, Wells, Fountains, and Gardens—Drains, Baths, and Aqueducts—Tokens, Seals, Weights, Scales, etc.—Arts, Crafts, Conveyances—Wine-growing and Husbandry—Potter, Smith, and Metal Work— Woven Fabrics, Spinning, etc.—Banquets—Hunting—Indoor Life of Women, Costume, etc.—Furniture—Civic Life, School Scenes, Writing Materials—Burial, Cinerary Urns, Sarcophagi, and Sepulchral Chambers.

A Dictionary of Classical Antiquities

Mythology, Religion, Literature and Art.

From the German of Dr. Oskar Seyffert.

With more than 450 Illustrations. Third edition with much additional matter. Imperial 8vo Cloth, 716 pages. Price $3.00 net.

COMMENT OF THE PRESS.

" In the new and revised edition of Dr. Seyffert's Dictionary English readers are offered what is probably the most useful single-volume work upon the subject of Classical Antiquities to be had. The present edition has been edited by Dr. Sandys and brought sufficiently to date to include the latest discoveries and theories. The articles Comitia, Music, and Theatre are examples of the incorporation of new matter."—The Dial.

MACMILLAN & CO., New York.

ERRATA.

Page 15, line 14, read *Kegan*.
Page 18, line 5 from bottom, read *Balaustion*.
Page 18, last line, read *S w i n b ur n e*.

www.ingramcontent.com/pod-product-compliance
Lightning Source LLC
Chambersburg PA
CBHW021537270326
41930CB00008B/1289